The PAINTED Bathroom

The PAINTED
Bathroom

Stylish transformations with paint, tiles, wood, and glass

HENNY DONOVAN

CREATIVE
PUBLISHING
international

CHANHASSEN, MINNESOTA

www.creativepub.com

Contents

6 INTRODUCTION

8 GETTING STARTED

24 COLOR

26 FINISHING & STYLING

30 Blues and Lilacs

32 Koi carp in silver aluminum leaf

36 Seascape mural

40 Damask walls

44 Soft vertical stripes

48 Variations

50 Aquas and Greens

52 Etched glass squares

56 Dolphin mosaic backsplash and hand-painted tiles

60 Modern Swedish style

64 Leaf spatter

68 Variations

70 **Naturals**

72 Relief shells on neutral squares

76 Limestone marble trompe l'oeil

80 Variations

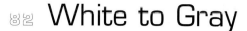

82 **White to Gray**

84 New England style

88 Geometric repeat

92 Calacatta marble

96 Variations

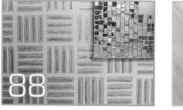

98 **Color Combos**

100 Striped shower curtain

104 Indian-style bathroom

108 Mediterranean floor

112 Variations

114 STENCIL TEMPLATES

124 RESOURCE DIRECTORY

126 INDEX

128 CREDITS

First published in 2003 in the USA and Canada by:
Creative Publishing international, Inc.

C CREATIVE
PUBLISHING
international

18705 Lake Drive East
Chanhassen, Minnesota 55317
1-800-328-3895
www.creativepub.com

President/CEO Michael Eleftheriou
Vice President/Publisher Linda Ball
Vice President of Sales and Marketing
Kevin Hass

ISBN 1-58923-073-6

Conceived, designed, and produced by
Quarto Publishing Inc.
The Old Brewery
6 Blundell Street
London N7 9BH

Editor Kate Tuckett
Senior Art Editor Sally Bond
Text Editors Jan Cutler, Gillian Kemp
Designer Julie Francis
Photographer Paul Forrester
Indexer Dorothy Frame

Art Director Moira Clinch
Publisher Piers Spence

Manufactured by Universal Graphics (Pte)
Ltd., Singapore; printed by Star Standard
Industries (Pte) Ltd., Singapore

▲ The stylish, graphic white and charcoal marble finishes in this bathroom have a clean, contemporary elegance with a timeless appeal. See pages 92–95.

INTRODUCTION

The bathroom is one of the most important rooms in the house in which to relax and rejuvenate. The general thrust of life these days is faster, busier, and more demanding than ever before, and time to recharge and unwind is precious. It is hardly surprising that we want the space we have created for those rare moments to be a special retreat, somewhere that will cause a feeling of well-being as soon as we enter it; a space that restores the senses, makes us feel renewed, and washes away the cares and stresses of the day. So the bathroom needs to look and feel good, which is why our focus has turned to its decoration and style. Decoration that is well thought out will create just the mood and atmosphere you want. *The Painted Bathroom* will inspire you to try out a totally new decorating scheme, to create your own personal bathroom retreat.

The bathroom lends itself to a multitude of decorative possibilities: walls, paneling, floors, backsplashes, tiles, soft furnishings, and bathroom furniture are all excellent surfaces to decorate. This potential, combined with a variety of different themes and techniques, provides all sorts of exciting possibilities for a completely new look.

The Painted Bathroom brings these factors together into a new, easy-to-follow guide with 16 exciting and innovative step-by-step projects and 20 variations, all illustrated with inspirational photographs, to give you all the decorating ideas and know-how for a complete bathroom makeover in contemporary or updated classic styles.

Color immediately alters the feeling and atmosphere of any room, making it at once invigorating, energizing, restful, calming, or healing. With this in mind, the book has been organized by color, each chapter demonstrating how to create the particular mood you want for your bathroom. An introductory section on color is also included to give you an insight into its uses.

▶ Working with the thematic approach of New England style, palest grey wooden panelling and a shoreline border stencil, this bathroom has a light, fresh and clean feel. See pages 84–87.

Pattern is making a big comeback in the design and decoration of our homes. We are no longer content just with plain, minimalist walls, but seek character, depth, and interest that patterned surfaces create. I have designed the stencils used

► Warm, earthy terra-cotta shades are perfectly complemented by simple wooden accessories, giving this bathroom a rustic, old-world charm.

throughout this book to show just how to bring pattern into a wide range of decorative schemes.

The projects illustrate how the extremely versatile decorative medium of design-based stencils in both modern and traditional pattern motifs can be applied to walls, floors, tiles, glass, fabrics, and furniture. Stenciling has been used to create allover pattern repeats, for example an 18th-century damask effect, as well as a modern, simple, geometric repeat. It has also been used to create a large koi carp mural in silver aluminum leaf, as well as for tile repeats on floors, beautiful spattered designs on tiles and mirror frames, subtle relief stencils, and a faux mosaic backsplash, as well as etched designs on glass, border repeats, and printed motifs on sheer fabrics.

I have also used a thematic approach for some of the bathrooms. Working with themes is great fun and can be one of the best ways to create a unified style. Theme-inspired projects include a modern Swedish-style bathroom with thick wooden paneling and delicate printed fabrics, in a tone-on-tone monochromatic soft green color scheme; a New England-style retreat in tones of pale gray, ivory, and blue-tinged charcoal, with a shoreline border and tongue-and-groove furniture and paneling (shown opposite); as well as Indian and Mediterranean style bathrooms. Other projects include a rich azure and ultramarine hand-painted seascape, cool Calacatta and limestone marble finishes, hand-painted jewel-like tiles, and metallic walls with etched glass squares.

Finishing and styling is essential to complete the look. Baths, sinks, basins, faucets, mirrors, and accessories—in sleek chrome, elegant glass, ceramic, marble, and cast iron—are used throughout the bathroom sets to bring out the best in each design.

Before you start on your chosen bathroom effect, read the comprehensive introduction to planning and preparation to ensure your new, fantastic bathroom will be a stunning success, then go ahead and enjoy discovering *The Painted Bathroom*.

GETTING STARTED

Planning the decorative scheme

In the last ten years the bathroom has become just as important a focus in the house as the main living areas. There is virtually no limit to the style and look that can be achieved, and there are extensive choices for bathroom fixtures in traditional styles and with sleek, modern lines. Options for bathroom accessories and fittings also seem to be endless—with comprehensive ranges in brushed or high-shine chrome, elegant glassware, porcelain, wood, rattan, bamboo, plastic, and more. With such an extensive choice, it is logical that you will consider new and complementary decorative schemes. So whether you are starting from scratch, with a completely new look, or planning a makeover to an existing bathroom, anything is possible.

STARTING POINTS

There are a number of useful starting points and inspirations to draw upon when choosing a decorative scheme. Use the following ideas to get you going and bring out the designer in you.

Inspired by a theme

Taking a thematic approach to designing a scheme can be extremely rewarding, great fun, and one of the best ways to create a unified, holistic style, where the whole room and everything in it is brought together in the scheme. Sources for this might be cultural influences from the four corners of the globe, or specific period styles, or a combination of both.

◄ Rich, opulent pinks, purples, and oranges with gold and glitter highlights blend perfectly in this Indian border motif for an Indian themed bathroom. See pages 104–107.

If New England style and the cool, bright, airy feeling of North Atlantic light inspire you, plan a whole theme around it. Old-world charm can be given a fresh, clean, modern feel, with wood painted in varying intensities of cool, neutral whites with splashes of color. Add bleached wooden frames, soft neutral towels, and all things natural, plucked from the outdoors.

If you love the exotic opulence of Indian fabrics, patterns, textures, and colors, try this as a theme for a romantic bathroom. Several bright colors and intricate pattern motifs can be combined with rich silks, gold accents, and dark, polished wood to create an exciting, yet intimate look.

Alternatively, try themes inspired by Mediterranean, Roman, French, Swedish, or Oriental styles, or by the Medieval, Victorian, Neo-classical, Regency, or Art Nouveau periods.

Inspired by mood or feelings

Modern-day decoration, where we attempt to create particular feelings and moods, reflects the attitude we hold toward our homes and the way we live our lives. Color is central to this. We know if we pick the right color it will create a particular atmosphere. So we usually look at what we want to achieve first and then see which color corresponds to this feeling; even when we choose the color first there is an instinctive sense of what its effect will be. This is why color choices are subjective and personal—based on feeling, rather than merely knowledge of the science of color.

To create an atmosphere that will energize,

stimulate and invigorate, choose intense and bright colors. But rather than painting a whole room with them, use them more like color "vitamins." Use accents, accessories, and splashes of intense color, or perhaps paint just one wall.

To achieve a feeling of restfulness, balance, and rejuvenation, use pastel colors. These will give a feeling of space and are most effective as solid blocks of color, which produce a feeling of being bathed in the color. Add accents of richer colors and natural materials to anchor the scheme (see Color, pages 24–25).

Inspired by pattern

Pattern is integral to most design schemes: it gives depth, interest, and focus and is an excellent way of harmonizing different colors. Most decorative schemes—apart from very bare, minimalist designs—will have a pattern element, and even a plain-tiled bathroom has the geometric rhythm of the tiling itself.

Pattern falls roughly into four groups: geometric, motif, pictorial, and floral. Each group can be used widely in schemes for the bathroom, either singly or repeated, large or small.

Geometric patterns produce a sense of order and can be used either in repeat on tiles, walls, and floors or as strong features that will alter the feeling and proportion of a room—vertical stripes make rooms seem taller, horizontal stripes cause a space to appear wider.

A motif pattern can be either representational or abstract and can be used in diverse ways. It will link various elements of a room when used in repeat on different surfaces; or it can be featured on just one wall, or used as a border.

A pictorial pattern is generally representational and can be used very effectively on differing scales to create feature walls in the bathroom, such as on backsplashes or murals, or alternatively as an all-over repeat pattern.

Floral patterns create gentle detail and color—modern interpretations of simple leaf motifs are an excellent example of this.

◀ Close-toned soft greens create a calming and restful mood. See pages 60–63.

▼ Large ornate floral motifs are used in this repeat pattern—a modern take on classic 18th-century floral wallpaper. See pages 40–43.

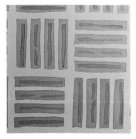

▲ Geometric—see pages 88–91

▲ Motif—see pages 72–75

▲ Pictorial—see pages 32–35

▲ Floral—see pages 64–67

◀ The four types of pattern—geometric, motif, pictorial, or floral—used either on their own or in repeated form, on small and large scales, create a complete matrix of pattern options.

Inspired by texture

There is an increasing demand for texture in our homes. Surfaces mean that we now consider texture as an integral part of decorative schemes, which gives tactile as well as visual possibilities. Shiny, smooth, silky, and sleek sit quite happily alongside chalky, velvety, grained, or coarse textures, whether on walls, floors, furniture, or fabrics, or a host of complementary accessories. Textured surfaces work on their own or with smooth, contrasting elements, and are ideal for use in the bathroom.

Texture can be found in painted surfaces—when shiny and matte surfaces are combined—as well as in textured paints and coatings. Some paint finishes give the impression of texture, such as colorwashing, dragging, combing, and distressing. Other paints are perfect for textured and relief effects such as impasto—where plaster paint or 3-D paint are applied thickly—and some have a built-in aggregate such as texture paint or suede paint (although suede paint is more suitable for a powder room than a bathroom). Plaster coatings, such as Italian marmorino or stucco lustro can be applied as a distressed or polished surface. And of course there are numerous textured wallpapers.

There are a variety of features to accompany these surfaces: the luxurious feel of cool, smooth marble, stone, and natural minerals, the sleek lines of chrome and glass, and a host of metallic finishes whose luster and reflective surfaces—whether in paint, varnish, or gilded effects—all provide further possibilities for creating textural contrasts. The more obvious smooth, shiny bathroom fixtures, and the effective use of mirrors also offer countless textural opportunities of their own.

Inspired by technique

There are some techniques and finishes that have a character and look that stand in their own right as starting points for decorative schemes, and which work well in the bathroom setting.

Classical or modern mosaic might be the source of your inspiration: its texture, its feel, and its pattern, constructed from many tiny segments of glass or ceramic. The specific decorative art form is the inspirational starting point here, with color and design choices as secondary considerations. Mosaic can be cleverly emulated using stencils—whether on floors or walls—as a backsplash, or decorative border.

Alternatively, you might find the effect of distressed painted paneling or a simple whitewashed floor particularly appealing—it's the appearance of the technique and the feeling that it creates that provides the inspiration. Otherwise, you may simply wish to create a marble bathroom, flexing your decorating muscles to design a unique, luxurious space.

▲ The texture of this distressed plaster effect, created using impasto or 3-D paint, is given extra luster with the sheen of a metallic varnish and accessorized with a more subtly textured sleek, silver mirror. See page 69.

▶ Real mosaic is cleverly emulated in this dolphin mosaic stencil—perfect for a sink backsplash; or create the look of a real limestone marble bathroom with this quality paint finish. See pages 56–59.

Room style and format

A bathroom can be a problem to plan imaginatively and effectively, simply because there are several large, fixed items that need to fit into a space that is often quite small, or an odd shape. All the plumbed-in features—such as the bathtub, sink, toilet, and possibly a shower or bidet—are permanent. Whether you are planning an entirely new bathroom or a scheme around existing fixtures, they ultimately determine the space available for decorative work.

If you are designing this room from the beginning, give careful consideration to the type of permanent fixtures you introduce, as well as its layout, because you will want it to look good for a long time. Although you can change the decorative finish, it's a far greater upheaval to change the main elements of this room.

To plan the bathroom layout, draw the room to scale on graph paper, including the position of doors, windows, and other fixed features such as plumbing, piping, and radiators. Also draw your chosen bathroom fixtures to scale on graph paper and cut these out to make mini-templates to move around on your room plan.

Try out as many layout options as the existing fixed features allow. Imagine how each option would work, taking into account the way the door opens, the position of any windows, and whether there's enough moving and standing space around each item. This is also the stage to plan out the positioning of any tiling and possibly tongue-and-groove paneling, which is great for hiding pipes.

Slightly raised floors are also useful for this purpose. Also consider whether any partitioning is needed to divide up the room and create a little more wall space.

When you finalize your design, leave it for a couple of days, then come back to it afresh to see if it still feels right and fits all of the criteria. You now have a basic layout around which to build your decorative scheme.

If you are restricted by the existing plumbing and your bathroom fixtures are in poor condition, or a dated, stale color, consider installing an inexpensive simple white bathroom suite—it might not be your ultimate dream, but it will dramatically improve the look and feel of the room and the impact that any decorative work will have. However, if you are stuck with your original bathroom suite, rest assured that a tremendous amount can be achieved decoratively. Vast improvements can be made with only a little imagination and flair, which this book aims to inspire and provide.

◀ The bath is given prime position in this bathroom with the sink and toilet fitted neatly and discreetly into the wall behind.

▼ Draw a scaled plan of the shape and fixed features of your bathroom. Cut out your bathroom fixtures, drawn at the same scale, and try out different layout options to fit with the room shape and fixed features.

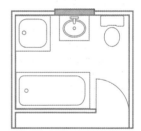

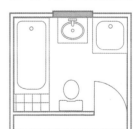

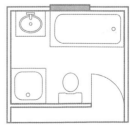

Choosing surfaces and techniques

As bathrooms are functional rooms, choose a decorative technique that will not only fit the style of your bathroom, but will also be practical for the amount of usage and the level of ventilation the room will receive. As bathrooms are subject to condensation and changing temperatures, good ventilation is essential. Large family bathrooms need to stand up to the robust wear and tear that heavy traffic and frequent climatic changes produce, whereas guest bathrooms have a far lighter usage. Seal decorative schemes well to improve the longevity of the finish.

The bathroom provides many different surfaces to decorate, including walls, floors, bath panels, cabinets, frames, bathroom furniture, mirrors, curtains, and shower curtains. You can plan a decorative scheme that will dramatically change the whole room or select specific areas to add extra quality and character.

Walls

Decorating the walls will have the most impact on the bathroom. Possibilities are far-reaching in terms of the techniques, styles, and colors that can be used. Consider decorating a feature wall, or adding detail to a specific area, such as a faux mosaic backsplash.

▲ Stenciled raised medium-density fiberboard squares stand out from plain paneling. See pages 60–63.

▶ Tongue-and-groove makes attractive furniture —here it is used as a New England-style cabinet, converted into a basin stand. See pages 84–87.

▲ Here relief shell stencils are applied to subtly contrasting, neutral-colored squares to make a stylish and elegant feature wall. See pages 72–75.

POSSIBILITIES INCLUDE:

- An overall color theme using a monochromatic palette, with subtle tonal differences between walls, bath panel, and woodwork; or a color scheme using different colors on different walls.
- Allover stenciled pattern repeat, either as an occasional single repeated motif or a continuous block of pattern emulating the effect of wallpaper.
- Feature walls and panels.
- Hand-painted or stenciled murals.
- Decorative detail to specific areas, such as backsplashes or decorative borders.
- Trompe l'oeil and marble finishes to give a sense of luxury and calm.

Tongue-and-groove

Using tongue-and-groove paneling on bathroom walls is practical and has a timeless appeal. It gives both a feeling of calm and space—even in small areas—and a homey feel. Use it vertically or horizontally, covering part of the wall—up to chair-rail height—or up to ceiling height to create a cool, lofty feeling. Associated with Swedish, New England, and Shaker styles, it can be used to create both a modern or traditional setting.

Doors, woodwork, and furniture

Painting doors, woodwork, and furniture will accentuate them as specific features or as accents of color and pattern to a main theme.

Floors

Painting floors is an inexpensive way to transform a room, often altering impressions of size and dimension. The best surfaces for painted floors are floorboards, hardboard, or medium-density fiberboard. Providing the surface is well sealed and protected with floor varnish it should give sustained usage (see Varnishes and finishes for the bathroom, page 26.) Bathrooms provide a well-defined, contained, and manageable space to attempt a hand-painted floor finish.

POSSIBILITIES INCLUDE:

- Pale washes for a bleached, whitewashed, weathered, and cool finish.
- Transparent finishes emulating the rich, woody tones of inlay and marquetry.
- Solid opaque paint—New England-style white floors.
- Simple checkerboard finish—Swedish-style, squares or diamonds.
- Pattern repeats and borders.
- Faux mosaic using stencils.
- Stenciled tile designs.
- Marbled effects, in large tiles or slabs.

Tiles and glass

Specialty porcelain paints can be stenciled, sponged or hand-painted on loose tiles and subsequently baked in a domestic oven before wall mounting. Glass accessories and ornaments can be decorated in the same way. Glass and mirrors can be given an etched finish using semi-permanent spray-etching paint.

◄ This stenciled tile repeat perfectly emulates the look of thick ceramic floor tiles in bright polychromatic Mediterranean colors.

Fabrics

Stenciling and hand-painting fabric can add a unique and beautiful touch to the bathroom. Fabrics can be made up into window curtains, shades, and shower curtains (hung with an inner waterproof liner) as well as cushion or seat covers.

POSSIBILITIES INCLUDE:

- Single-motif stencil designs as a simple repeat (see Dragonfly motif, page 48).
- Allover repeat stencils.
- Hand-painted stripes for a contemporary feel (see Soft vertical stripes, page 44).

▲ Here porcelain paints are spattered onto tiles in a simple leaf design to make a clean, stylish backsplash. See pages 64–67.

◄ Pastel colored stripes of different widths are hand-painted onto this sheer outer curtain to give a soft, yet crisp look. See pages 100–103.

Preparation

Preparation is a vital first step in decorating and plays an integral part in the quality of the finish. The bathroom, more than any other room in the house, is subject to dramatic changes in humidity and temperature levels, which have direct impact on decorated surfaces, and put an extra reliance on the quality of preparation to make the finish last. Proper preparation and careful basic decorating will mean that moisture will not get behind the paint and into the underlying plaster. Wood will be especially subject to expanding and contracting in these conditions, and therefore needs particular attention.

Allow plenty of time for preparation and priming and for base coat colors to dry thoroughly before any other finish is applied. This is known as 'curing' time and will mean that each successive surface treatment to be applied will adhere fully to the surface and have a longer life. The more time left between coats, the stronger and more durable the surface will be.

Dampness and moisture

As bathrooms are subject to condensation and changing temperatures, good ventilation is essential. If there are specific areas of dampness, these may have been caused either by lack of ventilation in a moisture-ridden atmosphere or by external problems. Residual dampness from external sources cannot be dealt with where it appears, as this will only cause the dampness to reappear elsewhere. The problem needs to be dealt with at its source, so it is important to seek professional advice. When the problem has been dealt with, treat the affected interior area with fungicide to kill mold spores (following the manufacturer's instructions).

The following charts show you how to tackle preparation for walls, woodwork, furniture, and floors.

PREPARATION OF DIFFERENT SURFACES

The basic principles to adhere to in preparing any surface are:
- Ensure the surface is clean and free from grease, dirt, and dust.
- Remove loose or flaking finishes.
- Fill any holes, blemishes, or cracks.
- Sand the surface to level out filler and to remove blemishes and bumps, and to create a key for the next stage.
- Wipe down the surface to remove dust.
- Size or seal as necessary.
- Prime or undercoat.
- Apply base coat.

BASIC EQUIPMENT AND MATERIALS FOR PREPARATION

Equipment	Materials
Cleaning cloths	Lint-free cloths, rags, decorator's sponges
Cleaning fluids, solutions	Diluted detergent; TSP (trisodium phosphate) solution; denatured alcohol (methylated spirit); paint thinner
Abrasives	Sandpaper and wet-dry sandpaper in fine, medium, and coarse grade according to level of sanding needed; flexible sanding block; steel wool; wire brush
Scrapers, strippers, knives	Broad-blade metal paint scraper; narrow-blade metal paint scraper; triangular shave hook; utility knife
Brushes	Natural bristle decorator's brushes; dusting brush
Sealing	White (PVA) glue or size for plaster, stain-killing primer for wood
Filling	Interior filler for walls and plaster; fine wood filler or putty for wood; frame sealant for gaps between plaster and woodwork; putty knife
Protective clothing	Overalls; aprons; rubber gloves; cotton gloves; face mask; safety goggles; ear plugs
Drop cloths	Cotton drop cloths, plastic sheeting, masking tape to tape down cloths

PREPARING WALLS

Wall surfaces	Method of preparation and materials
Newly plastered walls	Ceramic tiles can be applied to dry fresh plaster, but primer, latex paint, or wallpaper should not be applied for six months to allow plaster to dry out fully. Paint and decorative work applied too soon to new plaster will be subject to cracking. Traditional limewash may be applied, as it allows the plaster beneath to breathe. After appropriate drying, brush off dust or mineral salts, and apply size or PVA, diluted according to manufacturer's instructions. Leave to dry out completely, then apply a coat of acrylic primer.
Newly skimmed plastered walls	Walls that have had a new coat of skimmed plaster need to be left to dry for 2–3 days, or until fully dry, before sizing and undercoating with acrylic primer.
Old plasterwork	Old plaster may need some filling (see cracked plaster below), dusting or wiping down before sizing and priming. If the surface crumbles easily, apply a stabilizing solution before painting.
Cracked plaster or paintwork	Always repair and fill cracks before painting. Use a wallpaper scraper or blade to scrape out loose material from cracks or holes. Hairline cracks should be raked out to create a key for filler. Dampen areas to be filled with a decorator's brush and fill with appropriate filler according to manufacturer's instructions. Use a putty knife to press the filler into cracks or holes. When thoroughly dry, sand with fine wet-dry sandpaper. Wipe area with a damp cloth before priming.
Covered with new lining	If walls are papered with new lining paper, paint first with a thin coat of acrylic primer (50:50 water to paint), followed with a full-strength coat of primer.
Covered with old peeling paper, or paper unsuitable for painting	Paper that is old or peeling will not provide a suitable surface for painting. Do not attempt a "quick-cover-up," because it will not last. Wet paper with large brush or sponge soaked in hot water and score with a utility knife. Allow paper to soak for 10–15 minutes and repeat process. Use a wide metal scraper to scrape off the paper, being careful not to damage underlying plaster. Repeat until all traces of paper are removed. Alternatively use a steam stripper (available from DIY rental stores). Finally wash thoroughly with a scouring sponge, hot water, and detergent. Allow to dry. Any cracks or holes will need to be filled (follow filling instructions above). Sand filler and wipe down with a damp cloth, before priming with acrylic primer.
Covered with grass cloth or other textured paper or vinyl paper	Textured and vinyl papers consist of two layers. The outer layer of textured papers can usually be peeled and scraped off. Vinyl papers can usually be peeled off in whole strips. Start at the bottom, taking hold of both corners of the strip and pull away firmly, pulling upward. Remove the backing paper using the same method as above. If the backing paper is in really good condition, this can be used as a lining paper for your decoration, but do ensure there are no loose edges or corners (sand back).
Plaster painted with flat latex paint	If the surface is sound, remove any dirt and grease with TSP solution, and sand any rough or bumpy areas. Fill and sand any holes and cracks. Ensure area is free of dust. If you are covering a dark color with a paler color (e.g. pale yellow over blue or green, or white over red), prime the area first with white acrylic primer to ensure top color stays "true" and to assist good coverage.
Plaster painted with oil-based or acrylic eggshell or satin	Gloss paint that is to be covered with water-based paints needs particular attention, as water-based paint will not properly bond to shiny, non-absorbent surfaces. Remove dirt and grease with TSP solution, fill and sand any holes and cracks and sand the whole area thoroughly with medium-grade wet-dry sandpaper to create a key for painting. Wipe down with a damp cloth to remove dust and prime with an even coat of acrylic primer.
Lining paper previously painted with flat latex paint	If the surface is sound, remove any dirt and grease with TSP solution, and sand any rough or bumpy areas. Follow instructions above.
Lining paper previously painted with oil-based or acrylic eggshell	Providing the surface is sound, treat as a plaster wall painted with same treatment. Follow instructions above.
New tongue-and-groove (T&G)	Sand down wood and apply stain-killing primer to knots and resinous patches, to prevent discoloration to subsequent treatments. Fill any holes in the wood with fine wood filler and sand to a smooth finish, in the direction of the grain. Wipe off dust and apply two coats of acrylic primer, working it well into the joints.
Painted T&G previously painted with water-based, acrylic paint	Clean and sand with medium-grade wet-dry sandpaper. Fill any holes with fine wood filler and sand to a smooth finish. Remove dust and apply a good coat of acrylic primer. Strip thick and bumpy paint with an appropriate paint stripper. Sand and then apply an even coat of acrylic primer.

▲ Sand rough or bumpy areas

▲ Prime over dark colors with white acrylic primer

▲ Apply stain-blocking primer

Continued over page ☞

PREPARING WALLS

Wall surfaces	Method of preparation and materials
Painted T&G previously painted with oil-based paints	Clean and sand the whole area thoroughly with medium-grade wet-dry paper. Wash down. For uneven, flaking or blistered paintwork, scrape off or strip with an appropriate paint stripper. Sand down and fill any holes with wood filler. Sand and then apply an even coat of acrylic primer.
Bare, new MDF	Sand with fine-grade wet-dry sandpaper to a smooth finish. Apply one coat watered down white (PVA) glue (1 part PVA to 3 parts water). Follow with one coat acrylic primer. Make sure all cut edges of timber are sealed as well. Apply two coats of chosen base color.
Preparing a wall for tiling	Plaster in good condition is the ideal surface for tiling. Irregular plaster should be re-skimmed before applying tiles. A wall already tiled also offers a good surface, provided the tiles are firmly stuck to the wall and not chipped or broken. Use standard tile adhesive, but take care to stagger the new tiles, so that the joins do not line up with those underneath. Walls previously painted with gloss or latex paint are not suitable surfaces for tiling, as the tile adhesive needs to stick directly to the wall not to paint. Use coarse sandpaper to roughen the wall before tiling. Tiling should not be attempted onto any papered surface, as the tiles will only stick to the paper, which will not be strong enough to hold the tiles. Strip the paper from the walls before starting to tile.

▲ Apply tile adhesive to wall.

▲ Position tiles using tile spacers between tiles.

▲ Fill gaps with grout adhesive, removing excess with damp cloth.

PREPARING DOORS, WOODWORK, AND CABINETS

Doors, cabinets, furniture, woodwork	Preparation for washes or effects where wood shows through	Preparation for painted and decorative finishes
To prepare new, bare wood	Fill any cracks, holes, or blemishes with fine wood filler. Sand with fine-grade or wet-dry sandpaper in the direction of the grain of the wood until smooth. Apply stain-killing primer to knots to prevent discoloration from wood resin.	Fill any cracks, holes or blemishes with fine wood filler. Sand with fine-grade or wet-dry sandpaper in the direction of the grain of the wood until smooth. Apply stain-blocking primer to knots. Apply one coat of acrylic primer and two coats of base-paint color, taking care to paint the ends of cut timber.
To prepare wood painted with water-based or acrylic paints	Strip paint with appropriate paint stripper following the manufacturer's instructions. Wash off remains of stripper. If the paint is not too thick it may be possible to remove it using medium-grade or wet-dry sandpaper. Fill any holes or cracks with fine wood filler and sand the whole area with fine-grade or wet-dry sandpaper, following the direction of the grain.	Clean and fill any holes or cracks with fine wood filler. Sand down and prime with acrylic primer. If woodwork is covered with thick, bumpy layers of paint, strip back to wood with paint stripper. Sand and prime after stripping. Apply two coats of chosen base-paint color.
To prepare wood painted with oil-based paints	Follow instructions for stripping and preparing wood painted with water-based paints. You may however need several applications of paint stripper.	Wash down and sand thoroughly to create a key, then prime with acrylic primer. If original paint is uneven, flaking or blistered, scrape off or strip. Fill any cracks with fine wood filler. Sand and prime with acrylic primer.
To prepare wood previously coated with water-based varnish	Wash with diluted detergent, fill any holes or cracks with fine wood filler and sand with fine-grade or wet-dry sandpaper.	Wash with diluted detergent; fill any holes or cracks with fine wood filler and sand with fine-grade sandpaper or wet-dry sandpaper. Apply one coat of acrylic primer and two coats of chosen base color.
To prepare wood previously coated with oil-based varnish	Strip varnish with appropriate paint stripper following the manufacturer's instructions. Wash off remains of stripper. If the varnish is not too thick it may be possible to remove it using medium-grade or wet-dry sandpaper. Fill any holes or cracks with fine wood filler and sand whole area with fine-grade or wet-dry sandpaper, following direction of the grain.	Wash down and sand thoroughly to create a key, then prime with acrylic primer. If original varnish is uneven, flaking or blistered, scrape off or strip. Fill any cracks with fine wood filler. Sand and prime with acrylic primer, followed by two coats of chosen base color.
Bare, new medium-density fiberboard	Not applicable	Sand with fine-grade or wet-dry sandpaper to a smooth finish. Apply one coat watered down white (PVA) glue (1 part white (PVA) glue to 3 parts water). Follow with one coat acrylic primer. Make sure all cut edges of board are sealed as well. Apply two coats of chosen base color.

PREPARING FLOORS FOR PAINTING

Floor surfaces	Method of preparation
New floorboards for washes or stains	New boards that have not been stained and are clean should not need sanding. Scrub down with hot water and detergent to remove surface dirt and any dirt around nail holes. Leave to dry thoroughly. The floor is now ready for washes, stains, and varnishes. Apply wood bleach to decrease the yellowing effect of pine.
New floorboards for painted or decorative finishes	Follow instructions above. When the floor is clean and dry apply two coats of acrylic primer. The primer will allow the top coat to go on smoothly, to cover well and give a longer life.
Old floorboards for washes or stains	A floor sander will remove the previous layers of paint and varnish (see Sanding Floors). However, if the floorboards have a dark stain on them, consider the amount of preparation involved carefully before deciding on a transparent finish. Dark wood stain will have seeped right into the fabric of the wood and will prove very difficult to remove, even with deep sanding. Floorboards like this are best sanded and painted. Test a small area by sanding and rubbing back with steel wool and denatured alcohol: if the stain lifts, then it may be worth the effort of sanding the whole floor.
Old floorboards for painted or decorative finishes	Follow the instructions for Sanding Floors. Once the surface is smooth, clean and free from dust, prime with two coats of acrylic primer before applying your chosen base coat.
Medium-density fiberboard and hardboard for painted or decorative finishes	Medium-density fiberboard and hardboard can be laid directly onto existing floorboards. Ensure floorboards are flat and secure, with no protruding nails. Use boards that are 4' (122 cm) square, 3' (90 cm) square, or 4' × 2' (122 × 60 cm). Refer to a comprehensive DIY manual or get a professional to lay the boards (hardboard should be laid shiny side up). Hardboard must be conditioned (moistened) before laying, and medium-density fiberboard must be sealed with white (PVA) glue once laid. Prime either surface with two coats of acrylic primer before applying your chosen base coat.

FLAT PAINTING WALLS

The quality of decorative finishes is largely dependent on the surface they are applied to. A well-painted wall provides this surface. Use a paintbrush wherever possible, as this will give a smooth surface—a roller leaves a bumpy surface, unsuitable for stenciling or marbling. Follow these simple steps for correct flat painting, after priming.

◀ *Use as wide a brush as you can manage comfortably. Working in sections across the wall, apply a generous amount of paint to the wall, and spread across the area in large crisscross strokes, until the paint is evenly distributed. This process is known as "laying on."*

◀ *Then brush upward and downward through the paint in long, vertical strokes, creating as smooth a surface as possible. This process is known as "laying off."*

SANDING FLOORS

Equipment	Electric floor sander; edging sander (from DIY rental stores); sanding belts (in coarse, medium, and fine grade); nail punch and claw hammer; steel wool; denatured alcohol (methylated spirit).
Protection	Protective clothing; rubber and cotton gloves; face mask, and you may also want to wear goggles, to protect eyes from dust, and ear plugs, to block out the noise of the sander.
Making good	Punch all nails into floor to prevent tearing the sander. Remove old carpet tacks etc.
Removing wax	Some floors may have previous coats or patches of wax or polish. Remove with steel wool and denatured alcohol (methylated spirit) to avoid clogging up the sander. Wear protective gloves.
Seal room	Seal off room completely, using plastic sheeting and masking tape to cover doors and windows. Sanding is a very dusty process, dust will get into every nook and cranny of the house if not prevented. Where possible, leave a window open for ventilation.
Sanding main floor	Start near the edges of the room (slightly away from the wall to avoid damaging the baseboards). For a room needing heavy sanding, work the sander in diagonal lines across the room and then run it down the length of the floorboards. Never sand across the floorboards as this will gouge and damage the floor. For a room needing only light sanding work along the length of the boards, always lift the belt at the end of each run to avoid damaging the baseboard. Do not allow the belt to sit stationary on the floor while on, as this also will gouge the floor.
Sanding edges	Use an edging sander to sand up to the baseboards, taking care not to damage them.
Cleaning up	It is advisable to vacuum at regular intervals during sanding (some sanding machines have a dust bag attached) and very thoroughly after sanding is complete. Allow the dust in the room to settle for a couple of hours, and then vacuum again. Finally, use a lint-free, dry cloth to remove all remaining dust. It is better not to wet the floor at this stage, as water may mark the wood. The floor is now ready for your chosen finish.

Paints

All paint comprises a pigment, a binder, and a medium. Pigment provides color and covering power; the binder provides adhesion to the surface; and the medium makes application possible. The terms water-based and oil-based refer to the binder and medium and indicate which solvent is needed for thinning and cleaning. These are the two main and most widely used paint types. Wherever possible, water-based paints are used throughout this book, as they are far safer, more environmentally friendly, easy to use, and won't discolor over time.

Paints to use in the bathroom

Glossy latex paints are nonabsorbent and flat latex paint is absorbent. Decorative techniques, such as stenciling, stamping, and hand painting, are best applied to flat latex painted surfaces sealed with a coat of acrylic matte varnish. This gives a matte surface that allows the decoration to adhere and bond to the surface and will allow you to wipe off any marks without damaging or discoloring the painted surface. Shiny paints will cause the stenciling or stamping to glance off the surface, and to smudge, bleed, and fail to adhere properly. Once the decoration is complete a final coat of acrylic matte varnish can be added for extra protection.

Marbling and other techniques involving scumble glaze can be applied to semi-gloss or satin latex paint surfaces, but the paint must be applied very carefully to avoid ridges and brush strokes showing. Flat latex paint with acrylic matte varnish is an ideal surface for these techniques.

For general flat painting or painting wooden tongue-and-groove surfaces choose either flat latex paint, or wood paint with acrylic matte varnish for a more chalky finish or vinyl silk, mid-sheen latex paints, or acrylic eggshell for a slightly shiny surface.

The following charts give a brief description of the main primers, paints, and specialty paints which are used in this book (see Resource Directory, page 124, for suppliers).

PRIMERS, SEALANTS, AND TREATMENTS

Type	Description	Uses	Coverage per quart
Wood bleach	Caustic bleach solution for lightening wood.	Effective in eliminating yellow effect of pine. Used for treating floorboards.	As per manufacturer's guidelines.
Stain-blocking primer	A shellac-based sealing solution to prevent seepage from resinous areas.	Specifically for knots or resinous patches on new, untreated wood.	As per manufacturer's guidelines, but a little goes a long way.
Acrylic primer	A water-based primer, which seals surfaces and forms a key for other paints to adhere to.	Priming new or exposed wood, hardboard, medium-density fiberboard, new plaster, lining paper and as an undercoat for latex paint. For use on walls, ceilings, floors, and woodwork.	Up to 13 sq yd (12 sq m).

Coverage

When buying paint, be generous with your calculations and buy slightly more than you think you need. Never underestimate. Paint is made in batches, and colors may vary slightly from batch to batch.

HEALTH, SAFETY, AND ENVIRONMENTAL CONSIDERATIONS

• Keep all decorating materials and products out of the reach of children.

When working with paints and paint products:

• Always read and follow the manufacturer's instructions for all products.
• Always work in a well-ventilated area.
• Avoid allowing paint or paint products to come into contact with the skin and eyes.
• Wear protective gloves when working with oil-based and denatured alcohol (methylated spirit) based products.
• Wear protective gloves, mask, and goggles when sanding, using chemical strippers, spray paints, glues, or metallic powders.
• Wherever possible use products that are safe for the environment.
• Do not empty paints and solvents into drains or water systems.
• Where possible, take waste paint to the nearest household disposal site.

PAINTS FOR WALLS, CEILINGS, FLOORS, AND WOOD

Type	Description	Uses	Coverage per quart
Latex paint— flat or semi-gloss	Water-plus-latex-based paint. Higher quality matte versions contain more pigment and chalk, giving a less plastic look.	Painting walls and ceiling, can also be used on floors and furniture. Semi-gloss version not suitable as base for stenciling or stamping.	Up to 11–14 sq yd (10–13 sq m), depending on brand.
Bathroom and kitchen latex paint	Water-plus-latex-based paint designed for moist conditions. Mid-sheen finish, wipeable, hardwearing, but gives a plastic look.	Painting walls and ceiling, can also be used on floors and furniture—not suitable as a base for stenciling or stamping.	Up to 11–14 sq yd (10–13 sq m), depending on brand.
Metallic latex paint	Water-based latex paint for an allover metallic finish. Durable, wipeable finish.	Painting walls and can also be used on furniture and for decorative finishes.	Up to 11–14 sq yd (10–13 sq m), depending on brand.
Impasto, plaster paint or 3-D modeling paint	Water-based, thick paint for creating textured surfaces or relief stencils. (Can be homemade by adding powdered chalk to latex paint for textured finishes.)	Painting walls and as a decorative finish on wood or medium-density fiberboard. Can be colored with universal tinters, or colorwashed over.	Up to 4 sq yd (4 sq m).
Wood paint	A matte, opaque, water-based paint with built-in primer. High chalk and pigment content. Covers well. Better quality than latex paint. Should be sealed and protected with acrylic varnish.	Specially formulated for wood, furniture, and floors. Use full-strength for flat painting, distressing, and stenciling, or diluted for washes.	Up to 13 sq yd (12 sq m) undiluted.
Acrylic eggshell	Water-based eggshell paint with a satin sheen finish. Replacement for oil-based versions. Low odor and does not discolor over time.	Painting woodwork and furniture and as a base to scumble-glaze effects.	Up to 13 sq yd (12 sq m).
Oil-based eggshell	Oil-based eggshell paint with a satin sheen finish. High odor, will discolor with oxidization, but does flow well when applying.	Painting woodwork and furniture.	Up to 15 sq yd (14 sq m).
Oil-based gloss paint	Oil-based gloss paint with a gloss shine finish. High odor, will discolor with oxidization, but does flow well when applying.	Painting woodwork.	Up to 15 sq yd (14 sq m).

SPECIALTY AND DECORATIVE PAINTS AND MEDIUMS

Type	Description	Uses	Coverage per quart
Stencil and stamp paint	Water-based decorative paint generally flows better than latex paints. Available in flat, metallic, and glitter colors.	Suitable for flat latex paint, wood paint, colorwash, or impasto (relief) surfaces. Some brands also suitable for fabrics.	As per manufacturer's guidelines.
Tile paint	A water-based paint, which gives a semi-water-resistant finish.	Painting ceramic tiles in areas not subject to direct contact with water.	Up to 11 sq yd (10 sq m).
Porcelain and earthenware paint	Water-based decorative paint, suitable for baking for a durable, water-resistant finish.	Decorating ceramic, porcelain and earthenware surfaces. Good for decorating tiles before wall mounting.	3 tbsp (45 ml) will cover up to ten 4" sq (10 cm sq) tiles when painted as solid color.
Glass frosting/ etching spray	Solvent-based spray medium, semi-water-resistant finish.	Suitable for glass, windows, mirrors, but not for wet conditions.	Varies by application.
Acrylic scumble glaze	Water-based acrylic transparent, colorless glaze. Should be sealed and protected with acrylic varnish.	Used to create a wide range of paint effects. Also used for wood-graining and marbling effects. Dries to a satin finish.	Up to 17 sq yd (16 sq m), varies according to dilution.
Colorwash	Transparent, water-based glaze. Available either colored or clear for tinting. Should be sealed with acrylic varnish.	Designed for use on walls, also good for translucent stenciling.	Up to 33 sq yd (30 sq m).
Universal tinters	Concentrated, water-based tinting agent in liquid form. Disperses well.	Used to tint acrylic scumble glaze, clear colorwash, acrylic varnishes, thick textured paints, and 3-D stencil paste.	2–3 drops will adequately color 2 pt (1 liter) of scumble, clear colorwash, or acrylic varnish.
Gilding size	Water-based glue of milky consistency.	Applying Dutch metal, metal leaf, and metallic powders.	As per manufacturer's guidelines.

Equipment and tools for the job

Before starting any decorative project, gather all of the equipment you will need to complete the job successfully, so that everything is easily close at hand. The charts below show the basic equipment you will need for the projects in this book.

DRAWING AND MARKING EQUIPMENT

Equipment	Uses
Level	Vital aid to creating vertical and horizontal registration guides on walls
T-square	Angles, north and south axes on floors and walls
Tape measures 12" and 18" (30 cm and 45 cm)	Larger wall and floor measurements
Plastic rulers	Measuring, registering and marking up
Chalk reel	String in container of chalk for making registration guidelines
Masking tape; low-tack masking tape; painting tape	Masking off areas
Lining tape in ¼" and ½" (5 mm and 1 cm) widths	Masking tile and pattern repeats and for edging decoration
HB pencil	Drawing and marking (a hard pencil makes light marks, but press lightly)
Plastic eraser	Removing pencil marks

BRUSHES AND GENERAL EQUIPMENT

Brush/equipment	Uses
Low-tack masking tape	Masking off light switches, plug sockets, etc. when painting
2–4" (5–10 cm) decorator's brushes— natural bristle	Priming, painting latex paints, eggshells, gloss paints, and for general usage
2–4" (5–10 cm) decorator's brushes— synthetic bristle	Priming, painting, and varnishing latex paints, acrylic eggshell, and acrylic varnishes
2–4" (5–10 cm) varnish brushes	Applying shellacs and varnishes
Fitches	Mixing paints, for edges, moldings, and cutting in
Artist's sable brushes	Hand painting and detail, also application of gilding size to small areas
¼" and ½" (5 mm and 1 cm) one-stroke brushes in sable or nylon	Hand painting, good for creating clean edges. Nylon versions are good for painting on tiles
Stencil brushes	For stippling and fine spattering
Hog-hair softener	Softening, blending acrylic glaze effects (e.g. marbling), colorwash effects
Stippling block	Stippling glazes as grainy, veil-of-color or textured effects in thick paint
Natural sea sponge	Sponging broken glaze effects
Badger softener	Fine softening in glaze work
Decorator's steel float	Applying thick plaster paint (can also use a large palette knife)
Paint kettle	Mixing paint glazes and latex paints
Surgical gloves	Useful for glaze work, such as sponging
Tack cloth	Impregnated cloth for removing dust and particles, excellent for wiping down decorated surfaces before varnishing

Care of brushes

It is worth investing in good equipment and brushes. Quality brushes will improve with wear, as the tips of the bristles will become rounded, whereas the bristles in cheaper brushes tend to be poorly secured and will fall out during use. Your brushes will have a long life if they are well cared for. Avoid soaking for long periods, as this loosens the glue that holds the bristles in place. Wash promptly after use, to avoid paint caking in the bristles. Never let acrylic scumble glazes dry out on brushes, as the tips will be ruined for fine or soft work, and will be difficult to restore.

1 Remove excess paint with water, apply a little detergent to the bristles, and use a nailbrush to brush through the bristles and remove all traces of paint.

2 Rinse and dip in diluted fabric conditioner or hair conditioner to keep the bristles soft and in good condition.

3 Rinse and squeeze out, shake out excess water and leave to dry flat initially, and then hang, if possible, with the bristles pointing down.

STENCILING AND STAMPING EQUIPMENT

Equipment	Uses
Photocopy, layout, sketch paper	Sketches, designs and layouts
Pencils, black felt-tip pen	Drawing designs
Black permanent marker	Marking registration guides on Mylar®
Sticky tape and scissors	Sticking paper design to Mylar, cutting paper designs etc.
Mylar	Clear plastic sheets for cutting stencils
Craft knife	Cutting stencil designs
Metal ruler	Cutting straight lines in stencils
Self-healing cutting mat	Surface for cutting stencils
Repositionable spray adhesive	Securing stencils to all surfaces, prevents bleeding
Masking tape; low-tack masking tape, and painting tape	Masking-off around stencil, protecting edges
Paper plate or palette	Stencil and stamp paints (extra one for inking up stamp roller)
High-density foam in 1½" (4 cm) squares	Stenciling onto all surfaces, gives good application and control
Stencil brushes	Alternative for stenciling, though not as controlled
Paper towel	Dabbing off excess paint from stencil sponges
Mini-roller	Inking-up stamp
Ready-made stamp	Stamping motifs
Precut stencil	Stenciling designs

Stenciling techniques

Stenciling is an extremely versatile way to add pattern to a host of decorative schemes. Templates for all the stencils featured in the projects in this book can be found on pages 114–123. The stencils can also be purchased precut from the author's web-site— www.hennydonovanmotif.co.uk

Single motif design

Stencil design is based on the idea of cutting away shapes to create a positive pattern. This is done by creating a series of interlinking bridges between the cutout shapes that hold the design together. Although stenciling can be very intricate, the process involved is really not complex and it is possible to create your own stencil design with a minimum of drawing skills.

1 DRAWING YOUR MOTIF

Find a photograph or line drawing of an image you want to recreate. Trace over the main elements of the picture. Lay another piece of tracing paper or layout paper over your first tracing and start to separate the main shapes, incorporating the "bridges" between the shapes to be cut out. Work in pencil, and be prepared for a bit of trial and error.

2 CUTTING YOUR DESIGN

Photocopy your finished design and stick it onto the back of a piece of Mylar—a transparent film designed for stencils. Lay the design onto a self-healing cutting mat and use a sharp scalpel or craft knife to carefully cut away the main shapes of your design (or cut around your design if you are creating a reverse stencil). Use an even pressure to cut through the Mylar and take care not to cut through the bridges you have created in your design. It will take a little practice to cut out accurately the shapes you have drawn. Some shapes, such as circles and flowers, can be harder to cut, but designs with squares and rectangles, such as mosaic, are much easier to cut to start with.

◀ A design may have more than one layer, where extra detail is added on top of the first shapes that you create. These should be drawn within the first-layer shapes to ensure future registration, as shown in the design above. Registration dots can also be made in the corners, so that the two layers will line up—use a pencil to make registration marks when printing.

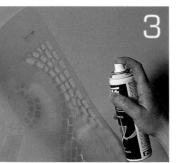

◀ A reverse stencil can also be created, which is where the cutout shape is used to stencil a negative image—this is ideal for etching.

3 SECURING STENCIL

Lightly draw some guide marks in pencil or chalk onto the wall to position the stencil. Use a ruler and level to ensure vertical and horizontal accuracy. Spray repositionable glue onto the back of the stencil and secure to the wall.

4 STENCILING YOUR DESIGN

To achieve good quality results stencil with a piece of high-density sponge. Pull the corners of the sponge together, dip into the stencil paint, and then dab off the excess on some paper towel. It is very important not to overload the sponge as too much paint will smear over the template and is likely to bleed beneath the design. Apply in light sweeping movements over the stencil.

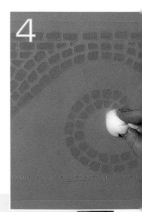

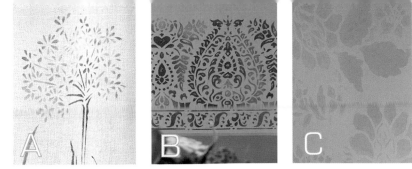

A **B** **C**

Repeat design

There are many types of repeat design. These include:

A Single motifs simply repeated in rows or columns, or in squares or diamond patterns.

B Border repeats where the design has a continuous linear repeat.

C Allover repeats where the design is adapted to flow continuously across the surface with no obvious joins—great for creating realistic wallpaper effects. This is done by simply inverting the design and adapting it.

Designing a continuous repeat stencil

Try out several designs and experiment with photocopying your design to see how the repeat works before you print. Designs with flowers and leaves adapt easily into repeat patterns.

1 Draw out your chosen design and trim the sides of the paper. Draw a vertical line down the middle of the design at points where there are or could be natural breaks. Label the left and right edges A and B. Cut carefully along this line.

2 Turn the two halves over and stick back to back, so that the left and right edges are now in the middle, as are the A and B. There will be an empty space left in the middle. Add extra motifs into this space to create a feeling of continuity. You may also need to rub out some elements of the original drawing to make it work.

3 Now draw a horizontal line through the middle of the design and label the two outer edges C and D.

4 Cut carefully along this line and stick the two halves back to back, lining up the two joins to make a perfect cross in the middle of the design. If the middle is not lined up in a cross, the design will not repeat correctly. A "step" may appear at either edge—this is a natural part of the design, so don't be tempted to try to make the edges line up. Add extra motifs to the center of the design, rubbing out any elements of the original drawing that no longer fit.

Positioning repeat designs

If you are applying a repeat stencil as a wallpaper style repeat you will have to deal with corners and creating straight vertical drops.

5 Photocopy the new design three times, cut out the design, and stick them together to check that they all line up for the repeat. It may take several attempts to get a design to work well, and in the early stages you may want to work with an outline drawing, getting it to repeat correctly and then adapting to a stencil design with bridges. With practice you will be able to draw out the design in the stencil format.

6 Make small registration dots in the corner of the design, if it is a two-layer design. Cut out following cutting instructions, step 2, Single motif design.

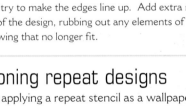

► Use a ruler, T-square, and permanent marker to draw two lines across the top and down the left-hand side of the Mylar. Use a level to make horizontal and vertical marks across the top and down the left-hand side of the wall.

Position the first repeat in the left-hand corner of the wall by matching the lines on the Mylar against the marks on the wall. The second repeat should then be directly under the first. Make vertical registration marks for the second drop and position stencil as for the first. Repeat this across the wall using the level to check that the design is straight.

COLOR

Color is the most powerful and inspirational tool you have when decorating. Throughout history, we have always made use of color in our homes; from the earthy pigments in early cave dwellings, to 21st-century paints available in literally any color.

The color of a room will affect you every time you walk into it, as color can alter the mood and atmosphere, making it invigorating or energizing; restful or healing; and so forth. The spectrum of colors available creates a spectrum of possible moods and feelings. This is why color choices are largely subjective, motivated by what you like, and what makes you feel good. Some people will feel invigorated by green, but for others, it might be blue or pink.

Color will be integral to your design decisions for the bathroom, right down to the color of the bathroom suite, even if it is just plain white. Your starting point might be a favorite color, or it might be a bathroom accessory that you could build a theme around. Conversely, you might be attracted to a decorating style that looks best in a particular color, or you may have a bathroom suite in a singularly uninspiring color that needs "knocking back" in the color scheme.

There is a huge range of possibilities available, which can sometimes make choosing color schemes a little baffling. Give yourself time to choose your color scheme: test the colors by painting samples onto large sheets of paper and hanging them up so that you can see how you react to them over the course of a few days.

Cool and warm colors

All color schemes derive from the basic relationships between colors. The color wheel is a helpful tool in understanding this relationship. It shows how the three primary colors (red, yellow, and blue) relate to the three secondary colors (orange, green, and violet) and the tertiary colors (where a primary is mixed with an adjacent secondary). Distinct cooler and warmer sides of the color spectrum can be seen, as well as the relative strengths of the different color intensities and tonal values.

Using warm and cool colors can create different moods. Cooler colors are known for their receding effect, making spaces feel larger and more airy. Warmer colors have the effect of advancing, and will appear to fill a space more. They are energizing and active, and also give a close-in feeling, which can be cozy and contained.

Blue *Green* *Violet* *Red* *Yellow* *Orange*

▲ Color wheel

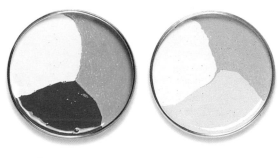

▲ Warm colors   ▲ Cool colors

Each color itself also has a cool and warm side. For example, there are warm, mossy greens and cooler sea greens; or cooler pale lemon and warm, sunny yellow. This can be used to great effect in altering the dynamics and atmosphere of a room.

Our association with the bathroom is that it should be a place to relax. For this reason cool colors are perennial favorites for bathrooms. However, brighter, more active colors—reds, yellows, and oranges—could be good choices for busy family bathrooms, to move the clientele on and out!

▲ Cool green   ▲ Warm green

Color and light

Light has a dramatic effect on color, so the quality of a color will depend on the quality of the light illuminating it. Daylight will create natural shadows and highlights, bringing out the different tones of a color, while artificial light has the opposite effect of flattening out colors. Normally, it is best to choose color in daylight, but if your bathroom has no windows, color-check in the room itself.

Color also has a definite effect on light, as different colors will reflect or absorb light at different rates. Lighter colors reflect light, causing the color to appear further away than it really is. Darker colors absorb light and so the color appears closer than it really is. It is useful to consider the size of the room, the source of light, and the effects of these on the color you are considering.

Colors that work together

The projects and variations in this book have been chosen to demonstrate how different color schemes and combinations work in the bathroom. Most color schemes are based on either synchronizing colors, or colors that work by their contrasting elements which are utilized to the full.

MONOCHROMATIC, TONAL PALETTES

Tone-on-tone, restricted monochromatic palettes make use of the different tones and intensities of a single color and create a unified scheme. A truly monochromatic palette will stay within either the warm or cool grades of a color. For example, purple or mauve moving toward the cooler, blue side of the spectrum, gives tones from pale lavender to deeper violet; whereas purple, on the warmer, red side of the spectrum gives more pinky tones of pale lilac through to rich purple. Green at the warmer end gives pale limes and moss colors (see Modern Swedish style, page 60), but at the cool end produces pale mint and aqua shades.

The monochromatic palette comprises a range of tones derived from an original color: light tones, known as tints (where white is added), and darker tones, known as shades (where black is added). The easiest way to use a monochromatic palette is to take a mid-tone color (such as green) and add successive amounts of white or ivory to obtain the paler tints. Mix three or four tones in total.

▲ Monochromatic tones of purple

Monochromatic schemes in neutral colors also work very well using tones of off-white, stone, taupe (cool), or ivory, pale sand, and honey-beige (warm). In this case, start with the lightest color, and then tint to the required shade by using differing amounts of raw umber, burnt sienna, and yellow ocher.

POLYCHROMATIC, COLORFUL PALETTES

Polychromatic schemes make use of different colors that share the same tonal value and intensity. A selection of colors with the same strength can have a natural color affinity, even if they are quite diverse. Modern brightly colored schemes make good use of this kind of palette (see Color Combos, pages 98–113), which is a contemporary take on more traditional schemes.

You can choose these colors by using small paint cards. Line up the corresponding level on each chart to see how the colors work together.

HARMONIOUS COLOR SCHEMES

Harmonious colors lie next to each other on the color wheel, so blend together decoratively. They work successfully using varying tonal strengths, so pale and stronger colors can be used here.

CONTRASTING COLOR SCHEMES

Contrasting schemes can be based on colors that have a stark contrast, such as black, or charcoal, and white, as seen in checkerboard tiles or striking marbles (see Calacatta marble, page 92), ultramarine and white, or colors based on more subtle contrasts, such as patterns in chambray blue and off-white (see Toile du Jouy variation, page 49).

COMPLEMENTARY COLOR SCHEMES

Colors that lie opposite each other on the color wheel are known as "complementary" or "opposite" colors. Schemes that use complementary colors work by using these contrasts. Complementary color schemes often need only a dash of one color against a backdrop of the other. These contrasts don't have to be painted; they can be added with accessories, flowers, or plants.

METALLICS With their ability to complement any color, metallics can appear quite neutral or act as a strong contrast. This is partly because of their reflective surface and partly because they have neutral colors beneath their luster. Silver is probably the most versatile metallic color, working with a multitude of different schemes.

▲ Polychromatic palette

▲ Harmonious palette

▲ Contrasting palette

▲ Complementary palette

▲ Metallics

FINISHING & STYLING

Sealing

It is essential to seal and protect decorative finishes in the bathroom carefully, to make your work last and to keep it looking good. Sealing will make the finishes moisture-resistant so that they will withstand the heavy wear and tear of the bathroom environment, including the regular wiping down of surfaces and frequent humid conditions.

This is particularly important in a bathroom that is used intensely, such as a busy family bathroom, as moisture can gradually work its way behind the paintwork and into the underlying plaster. In cases like this, apply an extra coat of acrylic varnish, and allow plenty of drying time between coats so that each coat has time to adhere fully to the wall before the next coat is applied. Also, ensure the room is well ventilated to disperse the humidity.

If the bathroom is used less, such as a guest bathroom with infrequent traffic, you may need only one coat of varnish. This is especially applicable if the room is well-ventilated.

VARNISHES AND FINISHES FOR THE BATHROOM

Type	Description	Uses	Coverage per quart
Metallic or pearlescent varnish	Water-based varnish with pearly, metallic luster. Gives medium protection.	For adding metallic luster to painted or bare wood surfaces. More suited for lighter colors, as darker colors can be difficult to cover smoothly.	Up to 17 sq yd (16 sq m).
Acrylic varnish	Water-based varnish available in matte (also known as dead flat), eggshell (also known as satin or semi-matte), or gloss finishes. Quick drying.	To seal and protect all water-based painted surfaces on walls, floors, woodwork, and furniture.	Up to 17 sq yd (16 sq m).
Acrylic floor varnish, also known as water-based polyurethane	Tough acrylic varnish specially formulated for floors.	Suitable for use over bare and painted floors.	As per manufacturer's guidelines.
Cellulose-resin-based varnish	An extremely tough two-part lacquer, with a resin catalyst.	For rooms receiving extra-heavy foot traffic.	As per manufacturer's guidelines.
Polyurethane varnish	Oil-based varnish in satin and gloss finishes. Adds a yellow luster to surface. Will yellow over time with oxidization. High odor.	For furniture, woodwork, and floors.	Up to 15 sq yd (14 sq m).

Walls and wall finishes

If a flat coat of color has originally been applied in bathroom paints, semi-gloss, or acrylic eggshell latex paints, varnishing is unnecessary. Walls painted in flat latex paint may, however, need a coat of water-based acrylic varnish for extra protection, although some flat latex paints do actually have a built-in sheen—test this by looking side on to see if the paint has a sheen, or alternatively wipe a small patch with a damp cloth to see how it reacts.

Use water-based acrylic varnishes on walls that have a decorative finish. Acrylic varnishes are strongly recommended for use in the projects throughout this book and are available in matte, eggshell, and gloss levels of sheen (see chart).

Acrylic varnishes are easy to use and dry quickly. They also have no odor and are non-toxic. They give a strong, durable, water-resistant finish, and they will not yellow over time, which is an

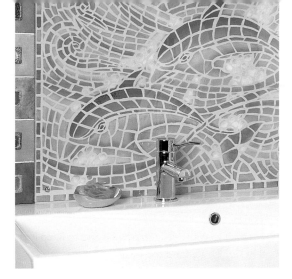

important consideration for decorative finishes for which you have taken time and trouble in putting your color scheme together. They also will not crack or chip in moist conditions in the way that an oil-based varnish will do in time.

Matte, eggshell, and gloss types of varnish are perfect for walls; although the eggshell and gloss varieties are recommended for walls that are to be wiped down frequently, as they have a higher degree of durability. It is highly recommended that all decorative finishes are wiped over carefully with a tack cloth to remove all dust particles before varnishing.

Polyurethane varnishes are not recommended for walls at all, because of difficulty of application, patchy finish, yellowing, and cracking over time.

Woodwork and furniture

Use acrylic eggshell and gloss to seal bare, unpainted woodwork and furniture. You can also tint the varnish if you want to "antique" or tone down the wood or add a little color to the finish. Alternatively use polyurethane varnish. Apply two coats of whichever varnish you choose.

Use acrylic eggshell or gloss varnish on woodwork or furniture that has a water-based decorative finish or a latex or wood paint finish. Do not use polyurethane varnish as this will discolor and spoil the appearance.

It is unnecessary to varnish woodwork or furniture painted with oil-based eggshell, satin or gloss (acrylic varnish will not adhere to oil-based surfaces).

Do not use polish or waxes on woodwork or furniture in the bathroom as they are not water-resistant and will mark every time they are splashed with water.

Floors

As well as using standard acrylic eggshell or gloss varnish on floors, you can use the special, tougher water-based floor varnishes that are now available, as shown in the chart.

The acrylic version of these is a tough, water-based polyurethane that can be applied either direct to bare wood or onto a decorated surface that has first been sealed with standard acrylic gloss varnish—this is to prevent any reaction between the painted surface and the water-based polyurethane varnish.

An even tougher option exists, which is a cellulose-resin-based varnish. The resin is added before application and acts as a catalyst to the cellulose base, creating a highly durable finish. Again it is advisable to seal painted finishes with a standard coat of acrylic gloss varnish to prevent any reaction between the painted surface and the cellulose varnish. Always read the manufacturer's instructions carefully before application.

It is not really advisable to use any kind of wax or polish on bathroom floors, because they are not water resistant, and will water-mark very quickly.

Gilding

Gilding can be used in a limited way in the bathroom to add a stylish finishing touch, but should be protected carefully. In the case of any decorative gilding on panels (see Koi carp in silver aluminum leaf, page 32), protect this from water with a sheet of glass or Plexiglas. It is inadvisable to have large, exposed areas of gilding (e.g. covering walls), because the metal will react to the damp conditions, and will discolor. Decorative gilding work on small objects, such as picture or mirror frames, should be sealed with white polish shellac and then varnished with acrylic or oil-based varnish in eggshell or gloss sheen. When embellishing small items with gilding wax, apply over a surface previously sealed with acrylic varnish, and keep away from water.

◀ To protect decorated surfaces from moisture, use a sheet of shatterproof, pre-toughened glass (at least ¼" [6mm] thick) or Plexiglas to cover the decorated area. Have the glass or Plexiglas professionally cut to size with holes drilled for dome-headed, plastic-protected mirror screws. Use a waterproof sealant around all edges of the glass. See pages 56–59.

▲ Delicate finishes such as gilding should always be protected by the method described above. See pages 32–35.

Styling and bathroom accessories

When planning your scheme it is wise to have an idea of the finishing touches you are going to use: will the scheme be best complemented with sleek chrome or will glass add extra definition and style to the look? Or would you like a more rustic or simple feel with wood or bamboo? Most decorating styles will be enhanced if you choose the right accessory to go with them.

The focus on bathroom design in recent years has meant that the choices for bath and utilityware, basins, sinks, faucets, and accessories are virtually limitless. Traditional styles have been given a high-quality lease on life, and innovative, sleek new designs have been introduced, accompanied by a vastly improved range of quality materials. To complement this, every imaginable accessory is available in a variety of materials. If you are planning to install a new bathtub, sink, and toilet, choose the style at the same time as you plan your decoration, so that the whole scheme works together. Similarly, if you are fitting new faucets or other fixtures, decide on their style before you start, to achieve an integrated final look.

▲ Ceramic bowl on reproduction washstand (top), wide square modern ceramic sink (right), glass bowl sink (bottom).

Sinks

As well as white ceramic sinks available in every imaginable style, including the elegant clean lines of simple square sinks, simple, neat bowls and basins are also popular. These attractive alternatives to the somewhat tired and cumbersome pedestal basin are available in a variety of finishes, including glass, frosted resin, stainless steel, ceramic, stoneware, and marble. There is a comprehensive range of shelves, countertops, and stands to complement them.

Bathware

Choose a bathtub from streamlined up-to-the-minute wall-fitted styles, or fashionable, modern, freestanding tubs. There are roll-tops for the 21st century or traditional, old-fashioned styles; there are also designer tubs in marble, glass, and wood, hi-tech Jacuzzis, and spa tubs. Good-quality tubs are available to suit all budgets, so you can choose either a style that will blend in with your overall scheme or else one that makes a strong statement in itself.

Most bathtubs are made from cast iron, steel, acrylic, or more modern stone-cast resin and are available in a variety of shapes, including rectangular, oval, corner, and hexagonal. Happily the fashion for strangely-colored bathroom suites seems to have faded into the past, and tubs are now usually a clean, simple white, suitable for most decorating schemes. Roll-tops have ready-to-paint exteriors, so that they can be tailored to decorating schemes, and an extensive choice of bath panels is also available.

▶ Reproduction cast iron roll top bathtub with claw feet (above) and modern steel bathtub in mosaic surround (below).

◀ Single monoblock lever

◀▲ Traditional tap and shower mixer (left) and modern, simple style taps (above).

Toilets and bidets

An assortment of toilets and bidets are available in styles that mix and match with all new styles and innovations for tubs and sinks, including modern, understated styles, and attractive reproductions.

Faucets

You can find bathroom faucets and mixers in types to suit all modern and traditional bath and sink styles. There are ranges of sleek, chrome faucets in clean, simple styles available as basin, bath, wall, and pillar-mounted single-hole, and three-hole sets. Color can be introduced by using attractive tap heads in frosted resin. Comprehensive ranges of high-quality, traditional designs are also available, as are showerheads and attachments.

Accessories and bathroom furniture

Mirrors, shelves, bath and shower racks, towel rails, towel rings, and toothbrush and toilet-roll holders are available in shiny and brushed chrome, brass, glass, frosted resin, porcelain, stoneware, and wood. They are designed to blend and harmonize with bathroom schemes or to stand out as design features in their own right.

Options for bathroom furniture are equally diverse. Choose from modern fitted cabinets and units in many styles and materials, or bathroom chairs, hampers, shelves, and storage units in rattan or wicker. Cabinets, freestanding units, linen presses, and armoires in painted or bare wood can also be considered. The range of options is endless—mix old with new, ornate with plain, or textured with smooth.

Add that finishing touch with soft neutral or colored towels, toiletries, and sundries that complement your scheme.

Painted bathroom projects

To accentuate the beauty or style of each scheme, the projects have been styled and accessorized with baths, sinks, basins, faucets, mirrors, and towel rails in materials that suit the style of the design.

◀▶ A deep freestanding roll-top bath has been painted to blend in with the soft greens of this project (left—see pages 60–63), while a beautiful travertine limestone basin brings out the beauty of the marble trompe l'oeil bathroom (right—see pages 76–79).

Blues and Lilacs

At the cool end of the color spectrum, blue and lilac create a palette that echoes nature's own diversity—the lilac-blushed dawn, watery gray-blue horizons, rich, clear skies, stormy blues, and deepest nighttime indigo, reflected in azure and ultramarine seas.

This multi-faceted range is a natural source of inspiration for decorative bathroom schemes. Blue gives a sense of balance and peace—a great color for rooms where you want to create a feeling of restfulness and relaxation.

Lilac is immediately calming and is said to promote tranquility and spirituality. Both colors are ideal for creating a place of retreat and contemplation.

From pale tints to strong shades, both blue and lilac work well with white, off-white, and silver. Use paler tones for a sense of spaciousness, and darker tones for a more contained atmosphere. As well as being individually versatile, blue and lilac work well together and can produce stunning results when combined with greens and grays, or enhanced with yellows, oranges, and pinks.

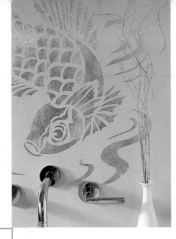

This beautiful and striking oriental-style koi carp design has been applied in silver aluminum leaf giving a really special, highly reflective finish. Excellent for rooms where you want a distinctive, high-quality feel.

Koi carp in silver aluminum leaf

Aluminum leaf gives an extremely opulent look here. As an alternative, the mural could be stenciled with brilliant silver spray paint onto a previously varnished base, or another color combination, such as blue on white.

Where to apply

This large, single-motif koi carp stencil is being used here above a sink most suited to a powder room or guest bathroom. For areas subject to more moisture it is advisable to cover the mural with Plexiglas (or thick, safe, shatterproof glass) to give further protection. The koi carp mural will also make a stunning feature wall elsewhere in the room.

Difficulty level: **moderate, although the gilding process can take a little time.**

YOU WILL NEED:

Koi carp stencil (page 115) • white acrylic primer • pale blue flat latex paint • acrylic matte varnish • acrylic gloss varnish • gilding size • white polish shellac • aluminum leaf—either loose or transfer leaf • decorator's brushes • varnish brush • gilding mop or soft brush • fitch brush • repositionable spray adhesive • palette or paper plate • high-density foam in 1½" (4 cm) squares • paper towel • medium grade sandpaper • level • Plexiglas, or safe, shatterproof glass (if necessary)

PREPARATION

The success of this project will largely depend on the care taken in your preparation, particularly in thoroughly sanding between coats, as the gilded effect works best on a smooth, flat surface. To achieve this, prime the wall with acrylic primer, sand until smooth and wipe off excess dust with a tack cloth. Then paint with two coats of pale blue flat latex paint, sanding and wiping off the dust between coats. Varnish with one coat of acrylic matte varnish.

1 MARKING UP AND STICKING STENCIL IN PLACE

Refer to Stencil Techniques (page 22). Use a level, ruler, and pencil to mark several points vertically down the central line of the area to be stenciled.

Use a permanent marker to make some small marks vertically down the center of the stencil. Apply repositionable spray adhesive to the bottom half of the reverse of the stencil and line up the central point of the fish with the central point of the wall according to the marks you have made. Stick the stencil to the wall. Firmly press all edges of the cutout areas of the stencil to ensure they are properly stuck down. This will minimize any bleeding.

2 STENCILING FIRST SECTION

Dip a piece of high-density foam into the gilding size and thoroughly dab off the excess onto a piece of paper towel. If there is too much gilding size on the sponge, it will bleed under the edges of the stencil, and the aluminum leaf will stick to this, causing the image to have blurred edges. Lightly stencil the gilding size onto the lower half of the stencil and then carefully peel off the stencil.

The gilding size has a sticking time of about 20–30 minutes, depending on room temperature. If you do not think you can gild half the stencil in that time, work in smaller sections at a time.

3 APPLYING ALUMINUM LEAF

You can use either loose leaf or transfer leaf. The transfer leaf is easier to handle, but can be more difficult to remove, while the loose leaf tends to be a little more difficult to handle, but is easier to brush away. The overall finish is the same, however.

To prepare the aluminum leaf, first wash your hands to remove any traces of gilding size and then lay out several complete sheets of leaf. Carefully cut some of the sheets in half using clean, sharp scissors.

Lift the leaf onto the sized area and carefully press down, smoothing out with a clean, dry finger to remove wrinkles.

Repeat this process until all of the gilding size has been covered, using the whole sheets for the head, main body section, and fish fins and the half pieces for the waves.

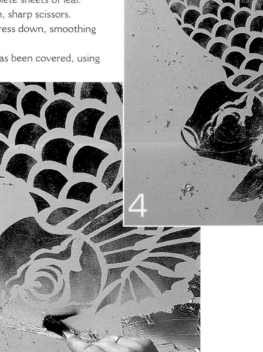

4 REMOVING EXCESS LEAF

Once all of the sized area has been covered, smooth your finger over it again to ensure the leaf is completely stuck down, and also to check that no bits of size have been missed.

Use the gilding mop or soft brush to brush over the gilded areas lightly, until the leaf that has not been stuck down starts to dislodge and the clean edges of the image appear. Keep brushing until all of the excess leaf has been removed. Carefully wipe away the excess. It is useful to have a vacuum cleaner on hand to clean up the metallic castings and dust.

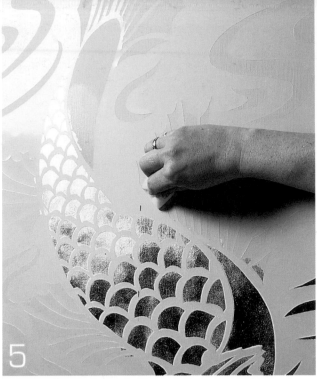

5 STENCILING SECOND SECTION

Apply repositionable spray adhesive to the top half of the reverse of the stencil. Use the original registration guides to line up the stencil carefully. Restick the stencil to the wall, pressing firmly into place, as before. Lightly stencil the gilding size onto the upper half of the stencil and then carefully peel off the stencil.

6 APPLYING ALUMINUM LEAF

Apply the aluminum leaf as before to the sized areas, carefully smoothing out each gilded section with your fingers to ensure it is fully stuck down. Repeat the process until the whole stencil is covered. When the gilding is complete, use the gilding mop or soft brush to brush off the excess aluminum leaf gently, as before.

Use a small dry fitch brush to loosen any stubborn pieces of leaf and to neaten up the gilded edges. Use some of the original pale-blue flat latex paint to cover any mistakes.

7 FINISHING

Use an eraser to rub off any pencil marks that are still showing. Brush off any loose pieces of eraser and then wipe over the whole surface using a tack cloth to ensure the surface is dust free.

Use a varnish brush to carefully apply a coat of white polish shellac, taking care not to over-brush the shellac, as this will cause a streaky finish. Leave to dry overnight.

Finally, varnish with two coats of acrylic gloss varnish. For areas subject to a lot of splashing, cover the area with a sheet of Plexiglas or safe, shatterproof glass.

This seascape mural will give your creative and imaginative spirit the chance to come to the fore, bringing crystalline, aquamarine, azure seas, and white sandy beaches right into your bathroom.

Seascape mural

More of an abstract painting than a beautifully drawn landscape, you do not need to be a full-fledged artist to get good results here. It's more a chance for you to create a space where you can relax and dream of far-off places.

Where to apply

This mural has been designed to run along the wall behind a bath, but it could equally be adapted as a stunning feature wall or panel. The mural is not suitable for shower areas (see Finishing, step 10).

Difficulty level: moderate, just needs confidence to have a go.

PREPARATION
Prime and then paint the walls in mid-blue flat latex paint, taking care to create as smooth a surface as possible. Varnish the walls with one coat of acrylic matte varnish.

1 SOURCE MATERIAL
You will need photos that have the stunning turquoise and blue colors so prevalent in the seas of the Mediterranean, Caribbean, and the Far East. You may want to paint a specific beach that you fell in love with on a particular vacation, or a more general inspiring beach scene—either way, collect together your seascape vacation photos. Additional sources could be postcards and pictures from travel brochures or magazines. Gather all of these into an inspiring montage.

2 WATERCOLOR SKETCH
Start the artistic flow by painting a watercolor sketch. Use the colors listed above in gouache or watercolor and paint a loose scene on watercolor paper, based on the scenes in your photos. Otherwise you could use my watercolor sketch as a starting inspiration

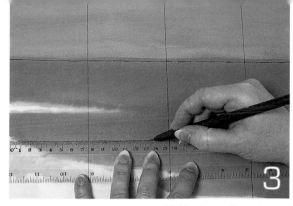

3 MAKING UP THE GRIDS

To enlarge your design you will need to create a grid both on your sketch and on the wall. The area of wall to be painted here is 4' × 3' (120 × 90 cm).

Trim your watercolor sketch so that it has the same proportional dimensions as the wall area. Then attach a piece of tracing paper and draw a 4 × 3 grid onto it.

Divide the wall area into a 4 × 3 grid. Stick ¼" (7 mm) lining tape on the vertical and horizontal lines to make up the grid.

4 TRANSFERRING THE DESIGN

Use a piece of white chalk to transfer the design onto the wall. Look at the horizon line and sketch in where it is in relation to the upper horizontal line (upper third), the sandbank (middle third) and the shoreline in the foreground (lower third).

Once the chalk sketch is in place, remove the lining tapes. You are now ready to paint.

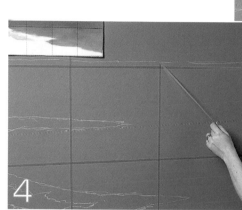

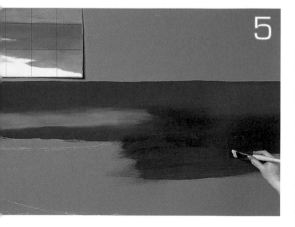

5 BLOCKING IN MAIN COLORS

A blank space can appear a little daunting, so the first stage is to block in all of the main colors. Use large fitch brushes and 2" (5 cm) decorator's brushes for larger areas. Start by painting in the main colors for the sea—ultramarine from the sandbank to the horizon, with a streak of turquoise above the sandbank. Then add Prussian blue to the right of the sandbank.

Now add a further line of ultramarine from the shoreline to the right edge of the mural. Paint in the remaining sea area with bright turquoise, and blend the wet edge of the ultramarine with the bright turquoise. Paint the sky in the same turquoise. Then paint in the sandbank and the beach area with the ivory acrylic paint, adding a splash of green to the sand dune on the left. You will have now blocked in all of the main colors and made a very good beginning to the mural painting.

Tip

To create a crisp line for edges on borders: stick painting tape or masking tape along the length of the edge; brush a thin coat of acrylic matte varnish over the edge of the tape, and allow to dry before painting. This will prevent any paint bleeding under the tape, and will give a clean, finished edge.

6 ADDING DETAIL

Add some more of the light turquoise onto the bright turquoise in the sea at the front just below the ultramarine band, blending the edges as much as possible. Add the same color to the skyline above the sea horizon line.

7 CREATING THE SHORELINE

Add more of the sandy cream acrylic paint to the sand dune and shoreline to create more textural qualities on the beach, and then add some green to the sand dunes.

8 APPLYING GLAZES

Follow the chart below to make up the two glazes for the next stage. These glazes will be semi-transparent and will have a longer open time than the latex paint base coats, which will allow you to blend the colors together.

Use a 1" (2.5 cm) decorator's brush or fitch brush to apply layers of the bright turquoise and sea-blue glazes to the sea, using the glazes to blend the light and darker blues. Use a hog-hair softener to feather the two glazes together and remove any streaky paint lines.

Use a 2" (5 cm) decorator's brush to apply two layers of the bright turquoise glaze to the sky. Use a hog-hair softener to remove streaky paint lines. On the final glaze brush over the horizon line, blending the sea and sky.

	Glaze 1: Bright turquoise	Glaze 2: Sea blue
1	2½ tsp (12.5 ml) acrylic scumble glaze	2½ tsp (12.5 ml) acrylic scumble glaze
2	1½" (4 cm) process cyan gouache, squeezed from the tube	¾" (2 cm) Prussian blue gouache, squeezed from the tube
3	Mix thoroughly to disperse paint and remove lumps	Mix thoroughly to disperse paint and remove lumps
4	2½ tsp (12.5 ml) bright turquoise flat latex paint	2½ tsp (12.5 ml) ultramarine flat latex paint
5	1 tbsp (15 ml) acrylic matte varnish	1 tbsp (15 ml) acrylic matte varnish
6	5 tsp (75 ml) water	5 tsp (75 ml) water
7	Mix and cover until ready to use	Mix and cover until ready to use

9 FINAL DETAILS

Once the painting of the sea is complete use a fitch brush to apply a little ivory acrylic paint to add definition to the top of the sandbank and sand dune.

Then use a little of the turquoise glaze, with some water added on a sable or one-stroke brush to run the color along the shoreline—this will soften the point where the water meets the shore.

10 FINISHING

If the mural is going behind a bath with minimum usage and will not be subject to a great deal of splashing (i.e. occasional baths only), varnish with two coats of acrylic eggshell varnish. For areas subject to more splashing, cover the area with Plexiglas (or thick, safe, shatterproof glass) to protect the mural. This finish is not suitable for shower areas, as water will get behind the Plexiglas covering and will mark the painted surface.

Give your bathroom a touch of style with this elegant damask-effect stencil and classic wood paneling in a modern lavender and metallic color scheme.

Damask walls

Subtle textural contrasts are achieved by using a highly reflective violet interference paint, which gives glimmering tones of silver and metallic violet—a damask shimmer on soft matte lavender walls. Interference paint makes the lustrous damask effect more obvious and once stenciled, it will appear silver at one angle and a vibrant metallic purple at another.

Where to apply

The two-layer damask stencil used in this project is designed as an allover wallpaper repeat, which can either be applied throughout or on selected walls above the paneling. The stencil can also be used for a full drop on one or more walls, but allow plenty of time for this. The paneling is perfect for lower walls, at sink height, or under sink units, as well as for bath panels.

Difficulty level: moderate, the repeat stenciling is quite a lengthy process.

Note

Tongue-and-groove paneling is not difficult in itself to fit, but creating a secure nailing strip system to attach the wood to and cutting wood to fit around doors, windows, and recesses can be difficult, and does require reasonable carpentry skills. I suggest you seek professional help in paneling the room, or if you are keen on DIY use a comprehensive DIY manual to guide you through the important stages. The face-nailing technique is explained in this project for enthusiasts.

Painted tongue-and-groove

YOU WILL NEED:

4" (10 cm) beaded tongue-and-groove timber to cover the area to be paneled • 1½" (4 cm) OG molding or chair rail to run across top of paneling • 6" (15 cm) baseboard molding for room or paneled areas only • wood filler • stain-blocking primer • denatured alcohol • white acrylic primer • lavender flat latex paint • acrylic eggshell varnish • acrylic matte varnish • decorator's brushes • fitch brush • 1" (2.5 cm) nails • nail punch • hammer • palette knife • sanding block • dusting brush

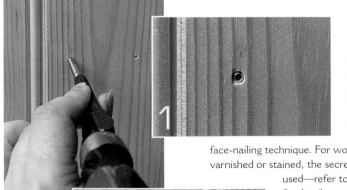

1 FACE-NAILING TECHNIQUE

This project uses 4" (10 cm) beaded tongue-and-groove paneling. As the paneling is to be painted, the tongue-and-groove boards can be attached to the nailing strips using the face-nailing technique. For wood that is to be left bare, varnished or stained, the secret-nailing technique should be used—refer to a comprehensive DIY manual for details.

Attach the tongue-and-groove boards to the nailing strip using small 1" (2.5 cm) nails. Sink the nail heads into the wood using a nail punch. Fill these holes with wood filler and sand when dry. Brush off any dust particles.

² ADDING MOLDINGS

The chair rail and baseboard moldings should be joined to the top and bottom of the paneled areas at this stage and prepared and painted in the same way as the paneling (see Finishing Touches).

³ PREPARATION FOR PAINTING

Once the wood paneling has been fitted, use a fitch brush to apply stain-killing primer to all visible knots to avoid any discoloration from resin. Clean the brush with denatured alcohol immediately. Prime the wood with one coat of acrylic primer. Make sure that you push the primer into the beaded joins to achieve full coverage.

⁴ PAINTING AND VARNISHING BEADED PANELING

Apply two coats of lavender flat latex paint to the paneled walls allowing plenty of drying time between coats for the paint to dry out in the beaded joins.

Make up a combined varnish mixture using ⅔ acrylic matte varnish and ⅓ acrylic eggshell varnish, and apply two coats to the paneled area. This will dry with a very slight sheen, which will complement the damask stenciled walls, but still have a near matte finish, particularly attractive on wooden paneling.

Damask stencil

YOU WILL NEED:

Two-layer damask repeat stencil (page 114) • white acrylic primer • pale lavender flat latex paint • acrylic matte varnish • acrylic eggshell varnish (if necessary) • violet interference paint for stenciling • violet metallic stencil paint • pearl stencil paint (if necessary) • repositionable spray adhesive • masking tape • divided palette or paper plate • high-density foam in 1½" (4 cm) squares • paper towel • level • ruler • pencil • plastic eraser • T-square • permanent marker • craft knife • hairdryer (if necessary) • tack cloth

PREPARATION

Apply one coat of white acrylic primer to the walls to be stenciled. Sand, and then paint with two coats of pale lavender flat latex paint. Varnish with two coats of acrylic matte varnish.

MARKING UP FOR STENCILING

Refer to Stencil Techniques (page 22). Use the ruler, pencil, and level to make guide marks horizontally along the top of the wall and vertically down the left-hand side of the wall. Use the permanent marker, T-square, and ruler to draw a horizontal and vertical line onto the stencil. If the stencil does not have registration dots in the corners, place the second-layer stencil on the first-layer stencil, so that all motifs line up, and cut registration dots in the corners.

¹ POSITIONING STENCIL AND STENCILING FIRST REPEAT

Spray repositionable adhesive on the reverse of the first-layer stencil and position the stencil in the top left-hand corner of the wall.

Spoon a good amount of the violet interference paint into a divided palette or onto a paper plate and apply using the high-density foam. You will need to apply three layers of the paint to achieve its full effect.

Apply a thin first coat of paint in light, sweeping motions over the stencil. Leave to dry. Apply the second layer using a little more paint, but wiping over the stencil in the same way. For the third coat, stipple the sponge onto the wall to create a slightly textured effect. Use a pencil to make a light mark on the wall through the registration dots.

To create a more obvious effect, stencil the first coat with the lavender paint used for the paneling. Then apply two layers of violet interference paint.

2 STENCILING REMAINING DROP

Remove the stencil and line up below the first repeat using the vertical marks on the wall and the line on your stencil. Place the stencil underneath the first motif so that the pattern motifs have the same amount of distance on the horizontal join as within the pattern itself. Use the permanent marker to draw around some of the flower petals from the first repeat that you can see through the Mylar. These will act as your registration guides. Press the stencil firmly to the wall.

Repeat the stenciling process as for the first repeat. Continue working down the wall until you have completed the drop, bending the Mylar up on the last repeat if necessary.

3 STENCILING SECOND AND REMAINING DROPS

Line the stencil up to the right of the first repeat so that the horizontal marks on the wall correspond with the horizontal line on the stencil. Position the stencil so that the pattern motifs have the same amount of distance on the vertical join as they do within the pattern itself. As before, draw some of the flower petals from the first repeat onto the Mylar, this time on the left-hand side, to act as registration guides for further repeats. You will now have drawn registration guides on both the left-hand side and top of the stencil. Repeat the stenciling process as before; remove the stencil, place directly beneath this repeat, and continue stenciling.

4 POSITIONING AND STENCILING SECOND LAYER

Apply repositionable spray to the reverse of the second-layer stencil and use the registration dots cut in the Mylar to position the stencil correctly. Press the stencil down firmly. Pour some of the violet metallic stencil paint into the palette and stencil using the high-density foam. The details on this layer should be subtle and not overstated.

Repeat this process until layer two has been applied to all the stenciled areas.

5 FINISHING TOUCHES

Rub off all pencil marks. The upper wall should not need varnishing again, as the metallic paint has a highly non-absorbent protective surface. However, for bathrooms with extremely high moisture levels, apply a coat of acrylic eggshell varnish, although this will reduce the contrast between the paints, giving the damask effect.

Finally, use some of the violet metallic stencil paint to paint lightly over the molding and skirting board at the top and bottom of the paneling. This attractive finishing touch will bring the whole scheme together.

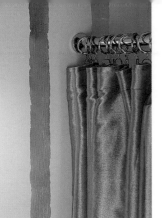

Create this simple, yet undeniably bold, striking, and modern look in several easy steps.

Soft vertical stripes

This project has the bonus of giving that feeling of extra height to rooms with low ceilings. It's great for a room where you want to create real impact.

Where to apply
Use as a striking feature wall or throughout a room.

Difficulty level: easy, but tearing the tapes is time-consuming so allow plenty of preparation time.

YOU WILL NEED:

White acrylic primer • mid-tone lilac flat latex paint • acrylic matte varnish • brilliant silver spray paint or silver metallic latex paint • painting tape or self-adhesive brown paper tape • wide low-tack masking tape • decorator's brushes • fitch brush • level • ruler • pencil • eraser • protective mask and goggles

PREPARATION
Prime and then paint walls with two coats of mid-tone lilac flat latex paint, taking care to create as smooth a surface as possible. Varnish the walls with two coats of acrylic matte varnish. The two coats of varnish used here will also act as the final coat.

1 MARKING UP THE WALL
Use a ruler and pencil to mark up distances of 2" (5 cm) and 6" (15 cm) horizontally across the wall to create the spacing for the vertical stripes. Use the level to ensure the marks make up vertical lines.

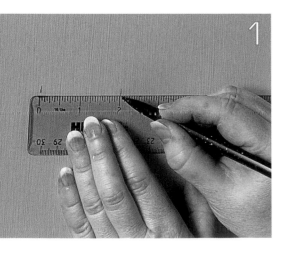

2 TEARING TAPE
Count the number of lengths of painting tape you will need to cover the wall, based on two per silver stripe. Cut the appropriate number of lengths of tape adding on approximately 2" (5 cm) to each length.

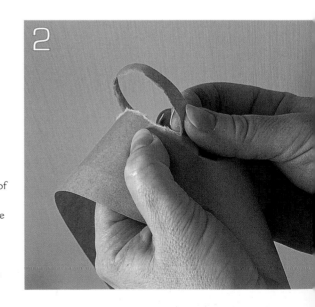

To tear the tape for creating the soft edge for the stripes, take the tape between the thumbs of each hand and tear a ½" (1 cm) wide strip off the sticky edge. Try to keep the torn line roughly straight, but do not worry if it is slightly wobbly or if you have to start the line again, the overall impression will be of a soft edge. You might want to practice on a shorter length of tape first to master tearing it.

3 ATTACHING THE TAPE

To stick the torn tape into place to create the outlines for the soft stripes, stick the tape to the wall so that the torn edges are to the left and right of each 2" (5 cm) stripe. You will find that as the tape has a torn irregular edge you cannot stick it directly onto the pencil marks—use them as a guide to keep the tape running straight. To ensure the lines are truly vertical, regularly place the level on the outer straight edge of the tape to check it is running straight and alter as necessary.

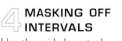

4 MASKING OFF INTERVALS

Use the wide low-tack masking tape (or more painting tape) to mask off the intervals between the torn-edge stripes. Ensure the lilac paintwork is covered to prevent any silver getting onto these areas.

5 ANTI-BLEED TECHNIQUE

Press the edges of the torn tape firmly onto the wall. Use a fitch brush to brush some acrylic matte varnish over the edge of the tape onto the lilac beneath and allow to dry.

Safety note
Always allow good ventilation while working.

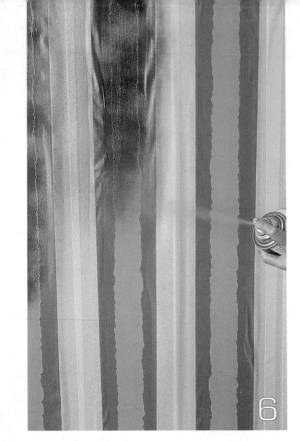

6 SPRAYING FIRST COAT OF SILVER

Wearing the protective mask and goggles and ensuring there is as much ventilation in the room as possible, spray the silver paint between the torn strips. Hold the can about 8"–12" (20–30 cm) away from the wall and spray a light film onto the wall. Shake the spray can vigorously at regular intervals to relieve any clogging of the nozzle. It is better to spray lightly over the same area repeatedly rather than attempting to spray a thick coat onto the wall, as that would cause the paint to run. As soon as you have finished spraying, leave the room, shutting the door behind you so that the fumes will escape through the window.

If you prefer not to use spray paint, a similar effect can be achieved using silver metallic latex paint. Although this will not have the odor problems, it will not create the same degree of brilliance. Silver latex paint will have a silver luster, which at many angles of the light will appear gray. The brilliant silver spray paint has a higher luster and does not appear dark from many angles.

7 SPRAYING A SECOND COAT

Allow the wall to dry for 30 minutes and apply a second coat of silver. Again spray an even, thin coat and build this up until a brilliant silver effect has been achieved. Leave the room again for 30 minutes.

8 REMOVING TAPES

Carefully peel away all of the tape on the wall to reveal the stripes. They will be brilliant silver, but with a pleasing soft edge.

9 FINISHING & STYLING

Allow the spray paint to dry for two hours, then use a plastic eraser to rub off any visible pencil marks and use a brush to remove any pieces of eraser. It is not necessary to apply a further coat of varnish as the lilac areas have already been varnished and the silver spray does not need varnishing. However, leave the paint on the wall to harden fully for 24 hours before using the room.

Further accentuate the textural contrast between the smooth, shiny silver paint and the soft matte lilac latex paint by using accessories that also have this implicit textural contrast—such as chrome and silver fixtures and fittings, metallic fabrics, and softer items such as towels.

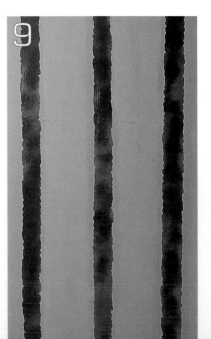

Blues & lilacs variations

Sea-theme paper collage

These collages are effective hung in groups on bright blue- or turquoise-painted walls. Tear strips of colored construction paper, wrapping paper, or paper from magazines. Use white (PVA) glue to stick onto firm backing cardboard. Use blue for the sky, turquoise for the sea, and beige for the beach. Add cutout details of boats or seagulls. Dry, and then trim the edges. Flatten under a weight for 24 hours. Stick onto medium-density fiberboard blocks or inside clip frames.

Dragonfly motif

Delicate motifs such as birds and insects are ideal on white cotton voile or painted walls. Make up a curtain (refer to Striped shower curtain, page 100, and to Modern Swedish style, page 60, for making up table and printing on fabric). Prime, paint, and varnish walls. Use pale blue stencil paint for the first layer, overprinting the wing tips with mid-blue. Stencil at 9" (23 cm) intervals to form a diamond pattern. Add a small leaf motif between the dragonflies. Stencil the second layer using cobalt blue.

Rope spirals

Textured silver spirals on pale blue walls are effective. Cut 10" (25 cm) and 12" (30 cm) lengths of ¼" (7 mm) rope/cord. Prime two pieces of 5" (13 cm) square cardboard. Apply a circle of adhesive to each. Wind the rope around itself and press into the glue. Seal the edge and center with white (PVA) glue. Make registration marks in a diamond pattern onto primed, painted, and varnished walls. Use silver stamp or stencil paint to print the stamps over the marks.

Koi carp and water lily mural

This is an example of how reflective metallic colors can create a stunning feature wall. Prime and paint the walls with pale lilac flat latex paint and seal with two coats of acrylic matte varnish. Position and stick your stencil onto the wall. Stencil your design using lilac and mid-green stencil paint; overprint with copper, purple, and jade metallic stencil paints (refer to Dolphin mosaic backsplash, page 56).

Contemporary squares

Harmonizing tones of purple create this striking design. Cut three sets of three wavy-edged Mylar squares in diminishing sizes. Paint the wall with rich purple flat latex paint. Stick the three largest squares in a vertical column on the wall. Seal edges with varnish. Paint inside the squares with lilac flat latex paint. When dry, stick three middle-sized squares inside the first, seal the edges, and paint with mid-tone purple. Repeat for the smallest squares using rich purple. Apply two coats of varnish to the wall.

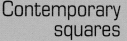

Toile du Jouy

This high-quality traditional scheme looks stunning both on walls and on fabric for shower curtains and blinds. The design is complex, but demonstrates the level of quality that can be achieved with stenciling techniques. Prime and paint the walls with ivory flat latex paint, and varnish with one coat of acrylic matte varnish. Stencil the whole design with denim blue stencil paint, then overprint the edges of the motifs to give depth. Follow guidelines for wallpaper effect repeat stenciling in Damask walls (page 40). Finally seal with one coat of acrylic matte varnish.

Aquas and Greens

The natural world provides a wealth of possibilities for bathroom color schemes. The first glimpses of spring, leafy glades, mountain streams, waterfalls, and ocean spray produce a refreshing sense of well-being and invigoration. The aquas and greens palette is both refreshing and invigorating, as well as healing and restful.

Aqua and turquoise evoke the feeling of water and its reviving properties. Pale shades create an atmosphere of spaciousness, and will be further enhanced by incorporating reflective glass and metallic finishes. Brighter tones will give a sense of richness and invigoration.

The green palette is naturally harmonious and restful. Use a cool, muted tone-on-tone scheme to create an atmosphere that will soothe and repair, or use zesty accents of lime to rejuvenate and restore the senses. Aqua and green have a timelessness and freshness that means they work well in both modern and classic decorative schemes.

This simple and effective use of glass, faux etching, and a metallic finish gives a contemporary feel that is both delicate and stylish. The reflective metallic and glass surfaces create a real sense of spaciousness in the room.

Etched glass squares

Three graceful etched feather motifs are repeated onto 12 glass squares and mounted as an elegant block.

Where to apply
This effect works best as a decorative panel or feature wall in the bathroom.

Difficulty level: moderate.

PREPARATION
Prepare the walls to be painted with metallic latex paint as thoroughly as possible to create a really smooth surface, as reflective metallic finishes show up any lumps and bumps. Prime the walls with white acrylic primer, then paint with two coats of pale aqua flat latex paint, sanding lightly between coats. Allow to dry thoroughly, and then sand again lightly.

YOU WILL NEED:

Feather stencils (page 119) • twelve ³⁄₁₆" (4 mm) thick polished glass squares each measuring 12" × 12" (30 × 30 cm) • twelve ¹⁄₁₆" (2 mm) thick medium-density fiberboard squares each measuring 12" × 12" (30 × 30 cm) precut at wood yard • white acrylic primer • pale aqua flat latex paint • pale aqua metallic latex paint or acrylic metallic varnish • pale turquoise flat latex paint • three cans glass etching or glass frosting spray • one can white matte spray paint • decorator's brushes • 4" (10 cm) synthetic paintbrush • ½" (14 mm) lining or edging tape • repositionable spray adhesive • denatured alcohol or glass cleaner • tube of extra-strong clear adhesive • strong bonding adhesive pads or fixings for 12 squares • sanding block • tack cloth • paper towel • newspaper or other protective paper • protective mask and goggles • craft knife • piece of high-density foam • level • ruler • book, or other weight

---

1 APPLYING METALLIC PAINT
Ensure the final surface is clear of all dust particles by wiping with a tack cloth. Use a 4" (10 cm) synthetic paintbrush (or as large as you can manage) to apply the pale aqua metallic latex paint. Metallic varnish can be used if metallic paint is not obtainable. Simply brush over the pale aqua paint base. Paint the wall in sections. Apply a generous amount of paint to each section.

Finish each section by laying off the paint in long, smooth, vertical strokes, working in one direction. All brushstrokes will show up on the reflective finish when it is dry, so finishing in one direction gives the smoothest finish possible. Allow the paint to cure fully for at least 48 hours before fixing the glass squares to the walls.

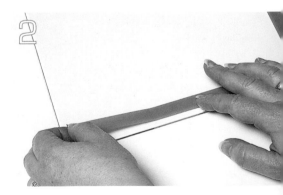

2 PREPARING GLASS SQUARES AND APPLYING TAPE BORDER
Clean both sides of each of the 12 glass squares using some paper towel and denatured alcohol or glass cleaner. Use the ½" (14 mm) lining or edging tape to create a border on each square. Stick the tape ¼" (7 mm) in from each edge, making sure that all of the corners are neat and that the tape is fully stuck down.

3 POSITIONING REVERSE STENCILS

Refer to Stencil Techniques (page 22). This project uses three different feather stencil motifs. You will need four finished etched squares of each motif. Spray repositionable adhesive onto the reverse of the feather stencils and stick in the center of each taped-off glass square. Take care to position the motifs the same on each square.

4 APPLYING SPRAY AND BUILDING UP THE ETCHED EFFECT

Work outside or in a well-ventilated room. Lay the prepared glass squares on newspaper or other protective paper. Shake the can of etching or frosting spray vigorously and, holding it about 12" (30 cm) above the glass, spray a fine even layer of etching spray over the glass squares.

At five-minute intervals, spray a further two coats of etching spray onto the glass squares, regularly shaking the can to prevent the nozzle clogging. To increase the opacity of the etched effect, spray a very light coat of white matte spray paint over the glass squares.

Repeat this whole process applying three more layers of etching spray and one more layer of white spray paint, leaving five minutes between coats.

Finally spray a further two coats of etching spray onto the glass squares.

5 REMOVING TAPES AND STENCIL MOTIF

Allow the glass squares to dry for a couple of hours and then carefully remove the tape and stencil motif from the glass; use the point of a craft knife to lift the tip of the feather and carefully pull the stencil away from the glass. To ensure the tape does not pull any of the etched effect away, carefully peel the tape back on itself, not at an angle.

6 PAINTING BACKING SQUARES

Backing squares are used behind the frosted glass squares to provide an easy surface to attach to the wall and to enable the etched effect to become more pronounced.

Use the sanding block to sand each of the medium-density fiberboard squares. Prime with a coat of white acrylic primer. Sand until smooth, and then paint with two coats of the pale turquoise flat latex paint. These squares need to have a smooth surface. To achieve this, paint the edges of the squares first, then rest the square on a slightly raised surface and brush in all directions until the square is covered. Carefully lay off the paint in even strokes working in one direction.

7 PREPARING FOR STICKING AND APPLYING GLUE

Leave both the etched glass squares and the backing squares to dry fully overnight. Ensure they are both clear of dust and particles. Then, working on four squares at a time, carefully squeeze a thin line of extra-strong clear adhesive around the outer edge of the backing squares. Leave this for 2–3 minutes to form a slight skin.

8 STICKING SQUARES TOGETHER

The glass squares are stuck down so that the smooth glass side is exposed. This will mean that the outer side is moisture resistant and the etched side is protected against the wall.

Carefully place the glass square directly over the backing square. Press down firmly all the way around the glass and remove any excess glue with a piece of cardboard or a knife. Cover each square with a piece of paper towel and place a heavy object carefully onto the glass to weight it down while the glue hardens overnight. Repeat the process for all 12 squares.

▼ Layout diagram

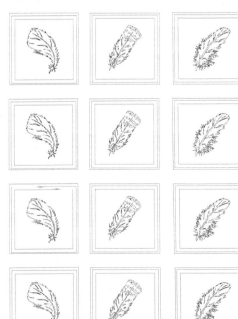

9 MOUNTING SQUARES ONTO WALL

Remove any fingerprints or greasy marks with denatured alcohol or glass cleaner.

Following the layout plan at left, attach the glass squares to the wall in a grid of 12, using either strong-bonding sticky pads or other glass fixings. Space the glass squares so that there is a 1¼"–2" (3–5 cm) gap between each square. Whichever size gap you choose (this may vary depending on the scale of the wall you are mounting them onto), ensure that each gap is exactly the same size throughout.

This stunning mosaic backsplash and tile effect has been created using a beautiful dolphin one-layer stencil and jewel-like, hand-painted tiles that imitate the expensive glass and metallic tiles that are becoming so popular.

Dolphin mosaic backsplash and hand-painted tiles

This effect will create a unique personal touch and high-quality finish at a fraction of the cost of real mosaic and store-bought tiles.

Where to apply

The stencil and tiles in this project have been designed to be used in conjunction with each other as a backsplash for a sink, but could equally be used as a mural above tiles on a feature wall, or the tiles could be used as part of a tiled wall in their own right—pick and choose to get the look you want. Specialty tile paints are used in this project, which means the finished baked tiles can be used in wet areas, making them especially suitable for walls and backsplash areas (although areas subject to constant wetness, such as showers, are not recommended).

Difficulty level: **moderate, although completing the project is quite time-consuming.**

BACKSPLASH

PREPARATION
Prime and then paint the walls with two coats of turquoise flat latex paint, taking care to create as smooth a surface as possible. Varnish the walls with one coat of acrylic matte varnish.

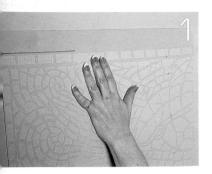

1 MARKING UP AND SECURING STENCIL
Refer to Stencil Techniques (page 22). Use a level, ruler, and pencil to mark up several points vertically down the central line of the area to be stenciled. Use a permanent marker to make some small marks on the stencil vertically down the center. Apply repositionable spray adhesive to the reverse of the stencil and line up the central point of the mosaic design with the central point of the wall according to the marks you have made, and stick to the wall. Use the level to check that the design is horizontal.

Firmly press all edges of the cutout areas of the stencil to ensure they are properly stuck down. This will minimize any bleeding.

2 STENCILING FIRST STAGE
The best effect with this design is achieved by building up layers of color to create the depth and richness of true mosaic.

Pour out a small amount of the stencil colors listed above into a divided palette or onto a paper plate.

Apply stencil paints using the guidelines in Stencil Techniques (page 22). Start with the white for the mosaic bubbles. Use pale turquoise and blue for the top and bottom parts of the dolphins, and pale green and blue for the water.

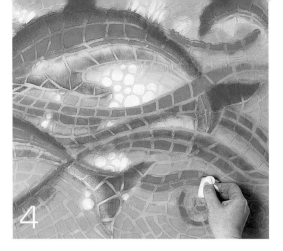

3 ADDING DEFINITION

Stencil bright turquoise to the tops of the dolphins' backs and more white and blue to the lower parts of their bodies to create light and dark shadows. Add orange to the line of mosaic running along the center of the bodies.

4 THE WAVES AND BORDER

Fill up the whole mosaic around the dolphins in blues, turquoises, greens, and a little lilac creating lighter and darker areas on the waves. Stencil the border using the colors you have used so far.

5 METALLIC COLORS

Pour out a small amount of the pale green, emerald green, sea green, pale turqouise, mid-blue, purple, gold, orange, and silver metallic colors, as well as some pearl stencil paint into a divided palette or onto a paper plate. Metallic stencil paint goes a long way, so you will not need much of each color. Stencil the corresponding metallic colors over the original colors. Add pale turquoise and mid-blue over the top of the backs, and silver and pearl to the lower bodies. Add metallic orange and gold over the orange stripe running along the bodies.

6 WATER AND WAVES

Add the metallic blues, greens, and pearl, and use the purple metallic paint to wash over some of the sea colors.

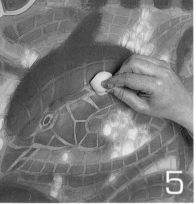

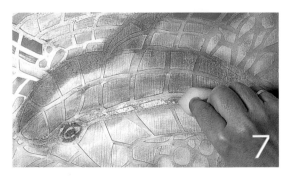

7 ADDING GLITTER HIGHLIGHTS

To add extra richness to the design, use stencil glitter paints in gold and sea green. To use the glitter paint, use a small brush to paint it onto your sponge and then stencil directly onto the wall. Build layers for a solid metal effect or stencil lightly for a dusting of glitter. Use sea green to highlight the dolphins' eyes and the top of their backs and gold for the line running through their middles and for some of the border.

8 FINISHING

Peel back the stencil to reveal the rich and diverse colors in your mosaic backsplash. Use an eraser to rub off any visible pencil marks. Brush off any loose pieces of eraser and then wipe over the whole surface using a tack cloth to ensure the surface is dust-free. Then seal the backsplash stencil with two coats of acrylic eggshell varnish. For areas subject to heavy splashing, cover the area with Plexiglas (or thick, safe, shatterproof glass) to protect the backsplash.

TILES

YOU WILL NEED:

Twenty 4" × 4" (10 × 10 cm) plain white ceramic tiles • porcelain paint in orange, turquoise, blue, green, and gold (see Resource Directory) • relief porcelain liner in gold, copper, and silver • glass gel paint in bright blue and iridescent blue • high-density foam cut to 1½" (4 cm) squares • waterproof adhesive • waterproof grout • palette knife • palette or paper plate • paper towel • artist's sable brush • small ruler and pencil • fine felt-tipped pen • 1" (2.5 cm) low-tack masking tape • denatured alcohol • level

PREPARATION

Clean the tiles with denatured alcohol to ensure a grease-free surface.

1 MARKING UP AND MASKING OFF

Use a fine felt-tipped pen and ruler to mark up a 1¼" (3 cm) square in the center of each tile—this will act as a guide at a later stage. Cut two pieces of 1" (2.5 cm) wide low-tack masking tape to fit exactly inside the marked-up square and stick securely. Mask off each tile in this way.

2 SPONGING FIRST COLOR

Pour a little bright orange porcelain paint into a palette and dip a piece of high-density foam into the paint. Sponge onto two of the tiles, covering the whole surface. Repeat this process for all 20 tiles using the turquoise, blue, and green porcelain paints. Apply the different colors to the tiles in even numbers, so that they can be paired when you come to mount them.

3 SPONGING SECOND COLOR

Allow the paint to dry for several hours, and then lightly sponge the gold porcelain paint in the same way over the orange. Handle carefully, as the orange paint will only be partially dry. Gold has been applied to soften the orange so that it blends well with the other colors and to give a metallic luster. Add a second coat of turquoise, blue, and green to the remaining tiles if you want to increase the color depth. Leave to dry for two hours and then carefully remove the masking-tape squares using a craft knife. Allow to dry thoroughly overnight.

4 APPLYING PORCELAIN LINER

Gold and copper porcelain liner is used on one tile, and silver and gold on the other. Gently squeeze the paste onto your premarked lines. Apply a second square, using copper inside the gold, and gold inside the silver. Allow to dry. For the gold and copper tile, apply further squares of gold and copper. When the liner forms a skin, dab a pool of gold porcelain paint into the tile center using an artist's sable brush. Leave to dry. Apply to all of the tiles, varying the colors used.

5 BAKING THE TILES

Place the tiles onto the oven shelf, and set the temperature to 300°F (150°C). When the temperature is reached bake for 35 minutes, then open the oven door and allow to cool. Follow the paint manufacturer's guidelines. You will find that the paste colors have blended and may have formed attractive bubbles on their surfaces.

6 APPLYING GLASS GEL PAINT

For the tiles with blank centers, apply the gel paint. Squeeze a small amount of bright blue gel into the central square and smooth with a palette knife. Remove any gel on the liner with a sable brush.

Leave to dry for a couple of hours and then apply the iridescent blue gel in the same way. Allow to dry overnight. The gel will dry to a hard resin.

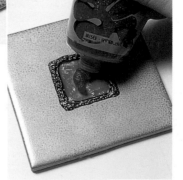

7 FINISHING

The finished tiles should be left for a couple of days to harden. They are then ready to mount around the mosaic. Use waterproof adhesive and grout, and a level to ensure the tiles are vertical.

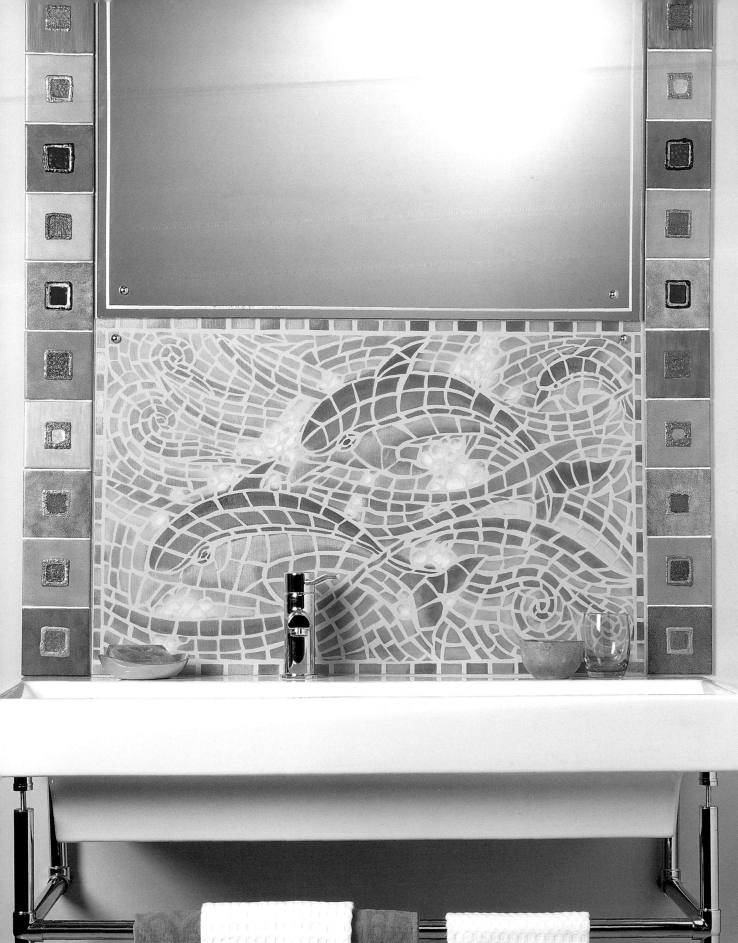

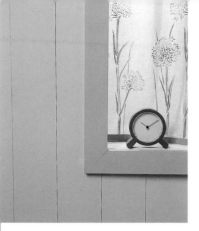

Create a calm, restful space with this modern Swedish-style bathroom where both traditional elements and simple, modern motifs and colors are combined effectively to create a harmonized and balanced feel.

Modern Swedish style

Thick flooring tongue-and-groove is used to create a truly Scandinavian look for the walls, and close-toned moss-greens give a sense of restful coordination. The delicate, hand-printed sheer fabric keeps the look light and airy.

Where to apply

This is a theme for the whole room—the wood paneling can be used throughout or on main walls and always looks good for bath panels, especially if you are not using a roll-top bath as here. The printed square pictures and sheer fabric can be used as feature items as appropriate.

Difficulty level: moderate.

Note
Refer to page 40 for advice on constructing tongue-and-groove paneling.

Painted Tongue-and-Groove

YOU WILL NEED:

6" (15 cm) flooring tongue-and-groove timber to cover the area to be paneled • wood filler • stain-killing primer • denatured alcohol • white acrylic primer • pale moss-green flat latex paint • acrylic matte varnish • decorator's brushes • fitch brush • palette knife • sanding block • dusting brush

1 PREPARING PANELING

This project uses 6" (15 cm) flooring tongue-and-groove with joints that fit snugly together. Once the wood paneling has been constructed on your chosen walls, fill and sand any nail holes or cracks in the wood (refer to Damask Walls, page 40). Remove dust with a dusting brush.

Apply stain-killing primer using a fitch brush to all visible knots to prevent future discoloration from resin. Clean the brush with denatured alcohol immediately after use.

2 APPLYING PRIMER

Prime the wood with one coat of acrylic primer. As the joins on the wood are close-fitting take care not to clog them up with paint, so apply the primer lightly over the wood joins. When the primer has dried, use the sanding block to lightly sand the wood to remove any roughness or small lumps that have come up from painting. Dust off with a dusting brush or dry paintbrush.

3 PAINTING TONGUE-AND-GROOVE

Apply two coats of pale moss-green flat latex paint. Before the paint dries, run a palette knife down the joins of the wood to remove any paint and keep them open. When the paint has fully dried apply two coats of acrylic matte varnish.

Decorative Squares

PREPARATION

Lightly sand each medium-density fiberboard square. Remove dust and prime with one coat of white acrylic primer, then paint with two base coats of pale moss-green flat latex paint. Allow to dry (refer to painting backing squares, step 6, in Etched Glass Squares, page 54). Using a ruler and pencil, mark up a 5½" (14 cm) square in the middle of each painted medium-density fiberboard square, and mask off the inner square using low-tack masking tape. Varnish the edge of the tape.

YOU WILL NEED:

Wild parsley stencil (page 118) • three ⅝" (15 mm) thick medium-density fiberboard squares each measuring 12" × 12" (30 × 30 cm) • mid-tone moss-green flat latex paint • pale moss-green flat latex paint • stencil paints in pale green, leaf-green, dark leaf-green, and ivory • white acrylic primer • matte acrylic varnish • decorator's brushes • fitch brush • sanding block • low-tack masking tape • painting tape • repositionable spray adhesive • divided palette or paper plate • high-density foam in 1½" (4 cm) squares • paper towel • ruler • pencil • tack cloth • screw eyes and picture wire

1 ADDING SECOND BASE COLOR

Once the varnish is dry, paint the outside of the squares, including the outer return, with two coats of the mid-tone moss-green flat latex paint.

Carefully remove the masking tape and varnish the whole of each square.

2 POSITIONING STENCILS

Refer to Stencil Techniques (page 22). This simple wild parsley stencil is designed as a continuous motif that carries on vertically over each of the three squares. To position the stencils, lay out the three painted squares in a vertical column, spray repositionable adhesive onto the reverse of each stencil and position them on each square making sure that the design lines up square to square.

3 STENCILING WILD PARSLEY MOTIF AND ADDING DETAIL

Pour a little pale green, leaf-green, dark leaf-green, and ivory stencil paints into a divided palette or onto a paper plate, and stencil the whole of each motif with the leaf-green. Apply patches of the pale green to the flower heads and some leaves on each square.

Stencil ivory onto the very tips of some of the leaves and around the edges of the flower heads on each square. When this has dried, stencil the dark leaf-green onto the very tips of the flower heads, the stems at the center of the flower heads, and some of the leaves.

4 VARNISHING STENCILED SQUARES

Allow each square to dry thoroughly and then varnish with one coat of acrylic matte varnish. Carefully attach two screw eyes to the back of each square and add picture wire for hanging. Otherwise, rout out a hole in the top center back of each square and hang.

Hand-Printed Curtain

PREPARATION

To make up a simple sheer curtain for printing, first measure the width and drop of your window. The width of the fabric should be 1½ times the width of the window; the length should be that of the finished drop plus another 4" (10 cm) for turning up a double hem at each end. When you have cut the fabric to the right size, turn the top, and bottom edges over twice. Pin, machine-sew the hem, and press.

1 STICKING FABRIC TO TABLE

Lay the bubble wrap and lining paper widthwise over a tabletop or counter and secure with masking tape. Use the ruler and pencil to draw a line ½" (1 cm) horizontally across the edge of the lining paper. Line up the bottom hem of the curtain with the line you have drawn, and stick the fabric down with masking tape.

2 POSITIONING THE STENCIL AND STENCILING FIRST REPEAT

Apply repositionable spray adhesive to the reverse of the stencil. Use a permanent marker to draw a line at the bottom of the design, line this up with the top edge of the masking tape, and stick the motif onto the curtain at the left edge. Pour a little pale green, leaf-green and dark leaf-green stencil paint into a divided palette or paper plate and lightly stencil the whole motif with the leaf-green.

Then stencil pale green onto the flower heads and leaves. Add the dark leaf-green to the stems and some of the leaves. Hold the fabric firmly and carefully peel back the stencil. Smooth out the fabric before positioning the next repeat.

3 STENCILING REMAINING REPEATS

Position the next repeat to the right of the first printed motif leaving approximately the same gap between the flower stems as in the design itself—this will give a feeling of continuity.

Continue the stenciling process, repeating the same colors on each motif until you have covered the width of the fabric.

4 FINISHING

To bring out the beauty of your hand-printed curtain sew a green trim to the bottom edge. Select a heading to hang the curtain, such as Velcro, tab tops, or no-sew curtain clips.

Roll-Top Bath

If you are using a roll-top bath, paint the sides in a toning green to fit the overall scheme or a contrasting color, such as black.

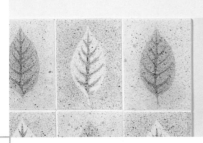

The combination of this beautiful, subtly toned tiled backsplash and decorative wide-framed mirror creates an atmosphere of simple cleanliness.

Leaf spatter

Soft greens and ivory are used here in a fine veil of spattered color and a simple leaf motif, which uses both positive and negative images. The result is pleasingly uncluttered and modern in its simplicity.

Where to apply

The tiles are ideal as a backsplash for a sink or would work equally well as a tile border or decorative tile panel. The mirror frame would lend itself to any appropriate placing within the overall context of this room theme.

Difficulty level: moderate.

PREPARATION

Prepare the wall to be used by first priming with white acrylic primer and then painting with two coats of pale green flat latex paint. When the paint has dried, paint a band of ivory flat latex paint around the wall. Use a level, ruler, and pencil to make guide marks for two horizontal lines, one at the top of where the tiles are to be mounted, and the other 3⅛" (8 cm) above the first. Mask off the rest of the wall with low-tack masking tape, and varnish to prevent bleeding. Paint the band between the tapes with two to three coats of ivory flat latex paint. Remove the tapes and varnish the whole wall with two coats of acrylic eggshell varnish.

Sand the mirror or picture frame. Use white acrylic primer to prime the frame and then paint the whole frame with the ivory flat latex paint, including the recesses and sides. Allow this to dry and then paint a pale green band at the top and bottom of the frame by sticking low-tack masking tape horizontally under the line created by the inner recesses of the mirror. Seal with acrylic matte varnish and then paint the upper and lower bands with two coats of pale green flat latex paint. Varnish the whole frame with acrylic eggshell varnish.

YOU WILL NEED:

Leaf stencils and leaf border stencils (page 119) • six 6" × 8" (15 × 20 cm) plain ivory tiles • a wide-framed wooden mirror or picture frame • mirror glass to fit frame • porcelain paints in white, mid-green, olive green, dark green, and gold • stencil paints in white, mid-green, olive-green, dark green, and gold • porcelain paint thinner • pale green flat latex paint • ivory flat latex paint • white acrylic primer • acrylic matte varnish • acrylic eggshell varnish • denatured alcohol • waterproof tiling adhesive and waterproof grout • decorator's brushes • fitch brush • stencil brushes • repositionable spray adhesive • painting tape • sanding block • divided palette or paper plate • high-density foam in 1½" (4 cm) squares • paper towel • disposable surgical or rubber gloves (optional) • plastic wrap • low-tack masking tape • level • ruler • pencil • newspaper or other protective paper • hairdryer (if necessary)

1 CLEANING TILES AND PREPARING PORCELAIN PAINTS

Use paper towel and denatured alcohol to remove any grease or dust from the tiles.

Pour a little of the white, mid-green, and olive green porcelain paints into a divided palette or onto a paper plate. Add the porcelain paint thinner until the paint has the consistency of light cream. Mix the paint and thinner using a small fitch brush. The paints are now ready for spattering.

2 ALLOVER SPATTER TO TILES

Place the six ceramic tiles on newspaper to protect surrounding areas. Use disposable surgical or rubber gloves to protect your hands while spattering. Spatter the mid-green porcelain paint mixture over the tiles by pushing a forefinger up through the bristles of the stencil brush. Repeat this process until the tiles are lightly and evenly covered with finely speckled color.

Using separate stencil brushes, spatter with the olive green and white porcelain paint mixture until the tiles have the effect of being covered with a fine veil of pale green. Cover the palette with plastic wrap and leave the tiles to dry.

3 POSITIVE AND NEGATIVE LEAF MOTIFS

Now spatter the positive and negative motifs onto the tiles—you will need three of each. Apply repositionable spray adhesive to the reverse of the positive and negative stencils and stick to the center of the tiles.

Add the gold porcelain paint to the palette and dilute with porcelain paint thinner. Spatter inside the positive stencil and outside the negative stencil with the mid-green, olive green, white, and gold porcelain paint mixtures until a subtle depth of color has been created. Remove the stencil motifs and repeat the process on the remaining tiles. Cover the palette with plastic wrap and leave the tiles to dry.

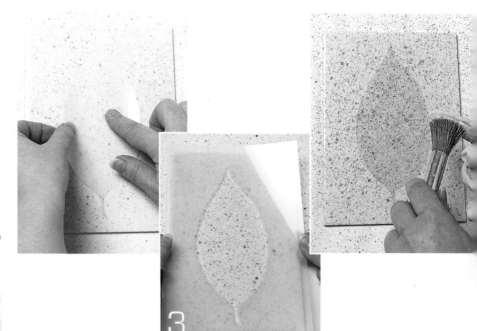

4 ADDING LEAF VEINS

Spray repositionable adhesive onto the reverse of the leaf-vein stencil and stick inside the positive and negative spattered leaf motifs. Use a piece of high-density foam to stencil some undiluted gold porcelain paint onto the leaf veins. Mix some of the dark green porcelain paint with the porcelain paint thinner and spatter the dark green through the veins. Repeat the process until the veins have been applied to all six leaf images. Put the tiles aside to dry for 24 hours.

5 BAKING TILES

Place the tiles directly onto the oven shelf of a cold oven. Set the temperature to 300° F (150° C) and bake the tiles for 35 minutes. Open the oven door and allow to cool before removing the tiles (follow the paint manufacturer's instructions, as these may vary for different brands).

6 SPATTERING THE MIRROR FRAME

Stick a line of low-tack masking tape around the outside rim of the mirror. Pour a little of the white, mid-green, olive green, and gold stencil paints into a divided palette or onto a paper plate and dilute until the paint colors have the consistency of light cream. Lay the mirror frame on some newspaper and very lightly spatter all over with a little of the mid-green, olive green, white, and gold color mixtures to produce a subtle film of color. Leave to dry for 30 minutes or use a hairdryer to speed up the process. To spatter the upper and lower bands of the mirror frame, mask off the central ivory section of the mirror with low-tack masking tape and use the mid-green, olive green, white, and gold colors to spatter these sections.

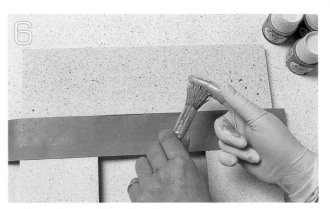

7 POSITIONING AND SPATTERING BORDER STENCIL

Spray repositionable adhesive onto the reverse of the first-layer border stencil and stick onto the lower band of the mirror frame. Cover the rest of the frame with paper and use the same colors to spatter through the first-layer border stencil to create a row of positive leaf images. Spatter until you have built up a subtle depth of color. Remove the stencil and repeat the process on the upper band of the mirror frame. Leave to dry for 30 minutes or use a hairdryer to speed up the process.

8 APPLYING LEAF VEINS TO MIRROR

Spray repositionable adhesive onto the reverse of the second-layer stencil. Position the leaf veins of this stencil inside the row of leaf shapes spattered onto the lower band of the mirror frame and secure well. Pour a little dark green stencil paint into the divided palette and dilute to the consistency of light cream. Add some more gold to the palette, but do not dilute. Using the high-density foam stencil the gold through the veins, and then carefully spatter some of the dark green through the stencil. Repeat the process on the upper band of the mirror frame. Remove the masking tape from the outer rim of the frame, and leave to dry out fully overnight.

9 FINISHING AND MOUNTING TILES

Varnish the mirror frame with two coats of acrylic matte varnish or acrylic eggshell varnish. Then use the ruler, level, and pencil to mark up the positioning of the tiles, just under the band of ivory you have painted on the wall. Apply waterproof tiling adhesive to the area where tiles are to be mounted and secure the tiles, following the manufacturer's instructions. When dry, carefully apply waterproof grout to finish the backsplash area.

Aquas & greens variations

Leaf motifs in colored rectangles

Contrasting greens and simple leaf motifs create this contemporary scheme. Prime and paint the wall in ivory flat latex paint. Mark up a block of nine rectangles measuring 9" (23 cm) by 11 ½" (29 cm). Mask with painting tape. Seal edges with varnish. Paint randomly with pale lime, peppermint, and pale moss-colored flat latex paints (refer to Relief shells on neutral squares, page 72). Seal with matte acrylic varnish. Stencil simple leaf motifs in rows across the rectangles using ivory and pale green paints. Apply a coat of varnish.

Mermaid and dolphins mural

This charming stenciled mural shows the pictorial effect that can be achieved using a two-layered mural stencil. Seal walls with acrylic matte varnish. Stick the first-layer stencil in position. Stencil—water: white, blue, green; dolphins: pale gray, blue; mermaid: green, gold, ocher. Overprint with metallic stencil paints. Remove, and position second-layer stencil. Stencil—water: as before; add metallic emerald to mermaid's tail; gold, and brown onto the shells. Finish with two coats of acrylic eggshell varnish.

Fantasy serpentine marble floor

Create this fantasy floor over two coats of ivory flat latex paint. Seal with acrylic eggshell varnish. Make up glazes by adding rich green and charcoal paint to the glaze mixture (use clear glaze recipe, step 1, page 92, Calacatta marble). Stencil a pale green, mid-gray, and pale gray geometric border around the floor. Apply a mottled effect in glazes (refer to step 2, page 93, Calacatta marble). Add vein lines in charcoal. Create a taped grid. Paint the large squares pale green, the rectangles pale gray, and small squares mid-gray. Varnish. Add a mottled effect and veins. Remove tapes, and varnish.

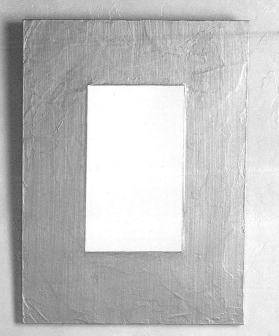

Distressed plaster with metallic finish

This finish is good for covering imperfect wall surfaces. Prime with acrylic primer. Paint with one coat of pale aqua flat latex paint. Use viridian artist's acrylic to tint impasto enough for two coats. Apply first coat with a decorator's steel float in a textured effect. When dry, apply a second coat by spreading some thick patches of impasto over the surface. Allow patches of first coat to show through. Leave to dry. Varnish with acrylic metallic varnish.

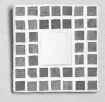

Spiral stamp variations

The simple spiral stamp is shown here in two variations. Paint the wall with two coats of turquoise flat latex paint, seal with acrylic matte varnish and stamp with white stamp paint. Alternatively, base-paint with white semi-gloss, colorwash with aqua, seal with acrylic matte varnish, and stamp with copper metallic stamp paint. Apply colorwash with a decorator's sponge in large figure-of-eight movements. Soften with a hog-hair softener.

Naturals

Tones of off-white, ivory, cream, and stone give a sense of calm and tranquility and a return to order—perfect for bathrooms for people who live busy lives or who just want to surround themselves with natural elegance and beauty. Natural-colored spaces feel light, airy, clean, and easy to live with.

Colors that emulate the look of plaster, natural stone, and marble create a cool modern, yet classic feel that can be dressed up to give a lived in, traditional look or dressed down for an uncluttered, minimalist style effect.

This versatile range of colors, with its inherent subtle differences, provides a wealth of decorative options and can be interpreted in both cool and warm colorways. Tones of off-white, stone, and taupe have a cool effect, whereas tints of cream, sand, and honey-beige add warmth and comfort. Cool schemes are enhanced by silver and sleek, brushed chrome; warm schemes naturally lend themselves to a touch of gilt and mellow gold. Use texture to add contrast, extra warmth, and interest.

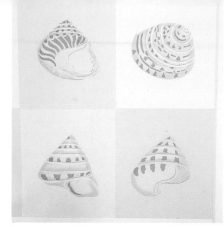

Subtle tone-on-tone neutral shades give this three-dimensional, shell-themed project a clean, contemporary, and calming feel.

Relief shells on neutral squares

Five two-layered single-motif stencils are featured here. The possibilities for variation and experimentation with different combinations of the five templates are endless.

Where to apply

This effect can be used in different ways, either as a feature wall in one section of the room or repeating the squares throughout the room with the relief shells appearing only in specific places.

Difficulty level: moderate, but requiring patience.

PREPARATION

Prime and then paint the walls in the ivory flat latex paint, taking care to create as smooth a surface as possible. Varnish the walls with one coat of acrylic matte varnish.

NEUTRAL RECTANGLES

You will need three more neutral cream latex paint colors, each one varying in either hue or tone. Along with your base color, these will form the four colors that will make up the painted rectangle base to the relief shells. For ease of reference label each latex paint *A*, *B*, *C*, and *D* (*B* being the original ivory flat latex paint).

1 MARKING UP
Refer to Stencil Techniques (page 22). Use a level, ruler, and pencil to mark up a grid using small pencil marks for rectangles that are 9" × 7" (23 × 18 cm). You can vary these proportions to suit your room.

2 MASKING OFF *A* RECTANGLES

Stick lengths of painting tape or masking tape around the horizontal and vertical frame of the whole area. Use your pencil marks to guide you and to keep the tape straight. Then stick painting tape (or masking tape) vertically to the left and right of the columns designated as column 1 (see diagram below), which will create three columns 7" (18 cm) wide. Now stick painting tape horizontally across these columns above and below your pencil marks to create the *A* rectangles. You will have now created six masked-off *A* rectangles ready to paint (see diagram below).

Layout of neutral rectangle colors

Column 1	Column 2	Column 1	Column 2	Column 1
B	C	B	*C*	*B*
A	D	A	*D*	*A*
B	C	B	*C*	*B*
A	D	A	*D*	*A*

3 PAINTING *A* RECTANGLES

The chart below gives the painting order. Use a fitch brush to apply acrylic matte varnish over the edges of the painting tape, to prevent bleeding. When this has dried paint the *A* rectangles with two coats of the cream flat latex paint that you have marked *A*. Remove the painting tape and allow the paint to dry.

Painting order		
A	Tape up and paint columns 1
B	Already painted
C	Tape up and paint columns 2
D	Tape up and paint columns 2

4 MASKING UP AND PAINTING *C* RECTANGLES

Once the paint is dry, stick painting tape or masking tape vertically to the left and right of the columns designated as column 2 (see diagram above), which will create two columns 7" (18 cm) wide. Now stick painting tape horizontally across these columns above and below your pencil marks to create the *C* rectangles. You will now have created four masked-off *C* rectangles. Varnish the edges of the tape to prevent the paint bleeding. Allow to dry, and then paint with two coats of the latex paint you have marked as *C*. Leave the vertical strips of painting tape, but remove the tape stuck horizontally across the columns and allow the paint to dry.

5 MASKING UP AND PAINTING *D* RECTANGLES

Once the paint is dry, stick the painting tape or low-tack masking tape horizontally across the same columns, but above and below the pencil marks to create the *D* rectangles (see diagram above). Apply varnish to the tape edges, and, once dry, paint the rectangles you have marked as *D* with two coats of latex paint. Remove the tapes and allow to dry.

Once dry, rub off any visible pencil marks, brush, and then wipe down with a tack cloth. Varnish the area with one coat of acrylic matte varnish. Leave to dry for 24 hours so that the paint can fully harden.

6 RELIEF STENCILING FIRST LAYER

Apply repositionable spray adhesive to the reverse of the first-layer stencils and stick to the center of each of the rectangles on the bottom row of the grid. Mask off the edges of the stencils with painting tape or low-tack masking tape. Use a palette knife to scoop a tablespoon of 3-D stencil paste or impasto onto the right edge of a decorator's steel float and smooth over the first stencil. Apply more paste and repeat until each stencil is covered with a medium-thick, ⅛" (3 mm) film of paste. Allow to dry and peel away the stencils very carefully.

7 STENCILING UPPER ROWS

Use the palette knife to remove the excess paste from the stencils and restick them onto five of the rectangles on the two rows above. Apply the stencil paste as before. Allow to dry, and carefully peel away the stencils. Wash the stencils and allow the first layer of stenciling to dry overnight.

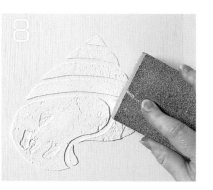

8 RELIEF STENCILING THE SECOND LAYER

Add two drops of raw umber universal tinter (or artist's acrylic or gouache) to the remaining 3-D stencil paste and mix thoroughly. Take a sanding block and lightly sand the edges of the dry relief stencils. Apply repositionable spray adhesive to the reverse of the second layer of the five shell stencils and position on top of the first layer.

9 APPLYING TINTED PASTE

Use the decorator's steel float or a palette knife to apply the tinted stencil paste. Repeat on the remaining motifs. Remove the stencils and allow the paste to dry out fully. Sand any rough edges when dry.

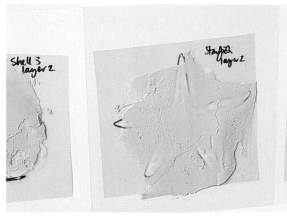

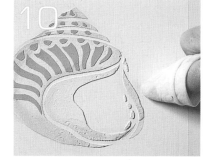

10 ADDING EXTRA TONAL DEPTH

Add two drops of raw umber and yellow ocher tinters to a small cup of acrylic matte varnish and mix thoroughly. Dip a piece of high-density foam into the varnish and carefully wipe it around the raised outlines of the shell stencils. Use a damp cloth to wipe off any varnish that gets onto the surrounding areas. The finished shells will have a subtle, but definite three-dimensional effect.

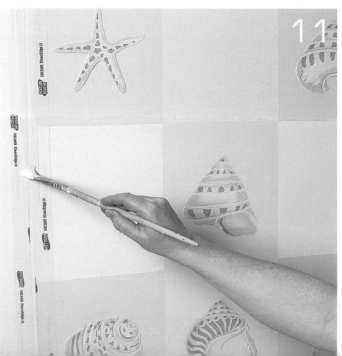

11 FINISHING

Use painting tape or low-tack masking tape to mask off a thin line running vertically down each edge of the rectangle grid and paint with the darkest cream flat latex paint tinted with a couple of drops of raw umber tinter. Allow to dry, remove the tape, and wipe down with a tack cloth. Varnish the whole panel with one coat of acrylic matte varnish.

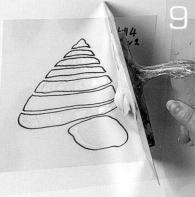

This classic marble-effect bathroom brings a welcome decorative solution to the increasingly popular fashion for all things limestone in the bathroom, at a fraction of the cost.

Limestone marble trompe l'oeil

Although you cannot paint a Venetian marble bath, you can create your own marble walls and floors. These are complemented by an architecturally drawn, aging trompe l'oeil mirror surround, which emulates the look of antique, molded plasterwork or carved stone, and adds a touch of historical beauty.

Where to apply

The ornate surround can be applied straight to the wall around a piece of mirror glass. The marble effect is very effective when applied over molded wood or plaster, as this emphasizes the natural lines and bands of the mineral deposits. Unsuitable for areas subject to high moisture.

Difficulty level: quite advanced, but the steps mean that anyone with enthusiasm can achieve good results.

PREPARATION
Use strong contact mirror glue to secure the mirror to the wall. Then cover the mirror with masking tape or paper to protect it. Marbled finishes need to be applied to very smooth surfaces, so take extra care in preparing the walls. Prime the walls with white acrylic primer, and then paint with two smooth coats of ivory flat latex paint. Varnish with one coat of acrylic eggshell varnish.

YOU WILL NEED:
Mirror surround drawing (page 121) • access to a photocopier • wooden molding or chair rail to fit your chosen area (optional) • medium-sized rectangular mirror • strong contact mirror glue • white acrylic primer • ivory flat latex paint • acrylic scumble glaze • acrylic eggshell varnish • raw umber, yellow ocher, sienna, white, and black universal tinters or artist's acrylics • vermilion, cobalt, leaf-green, Vandyke brown, yellow ocher, and white artist's gouaches or acrylics • decorator's brushes • hog-hair softener • badger softener • fitch brushes • artist's sable brushes and one-stroke brushes • soft varnishing brush (optional) • natural sea sponge • paint kettles • sealed containers • divided palette or paper plate • large sheets of 60 gsm tracing paper • drawing pencils • drawing fixative or hairspray • masking tape • protective paper • sanding block • level • ruler • plastic eraser • tack cloth • cream cleaner

1 DESIGNING MIRROR SURROUNDS
Design your own drawing for the mirror surround or use the template drawing on page 121. There are three templates for you to enlarge to fit to your mirror: one section for above the mirror, one section for below the mirror, and a section for the sides of the mirror. Alter the dimensions of the lines for the pillar effect either side of the mirror to fit your own mirror. Enlarge each section to the right scale and lay tracing paper over the three copies. Secure with masking tape and trace with a drawing pencil.

2 TRANSFERRING THE FIRST HALF
Use a level, ruler, and pencil to make a few horizontal marks to line your tracings up to the sides of the mirror. Position the tracings and secure with masking tape. Trace over firmly with your pencil, using a ruler to draw over the straight lines. Now redraw over the pencil marks. Use drawing fixative or hairspray to fix the drawing and prevent smudging. Continue until one side of the mirror surround is complete.

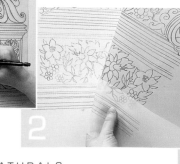

3. TRACING SYMMETRICAL SECOND HALF

Flip the tracings over and carefully line up with the first half you have drawn, checking that the tracings are straight. Secure to the wall and repeat the tracing and drawing process; apply drawing fixative.

Tip

Place a piece of paper under your hand while drawing to prevent smudging.

4. ADDING DEPTH TO DRAWING

Strengthen and thicken the pencil lines and shade some of the recessed areas to add more depth to the drawing. This will act as a guide when you come to paint in the details of this section.

Spray lightly with drawing fixative and remove any graphite smudges with a little cream cleaner on a damp cloth. Wipe away all traces of cleaner.

5. MIXING FIRST GLAZES

You will need a creamy-gray glaze and a buff, sandy glaze for the marble background. First make up approximately 1¾ pints (1 liter) of clear glaze using one-third each of acrylic scumble glaze, acrylic eggshell varnish, and water.

Pour about 3½ fl oz (100 ml) of this mixture into a sealed container and set aside for later, and then divide the remainder into two paint kettles. Tint these according to the following guidelines and mix thoroughly:

Creamy-gray glaze	Buff, sandy glaze
1 drop black tinter	4 drops yellow ocher tinter
6 drops white tinter	1 drop raw umber
1 tbsp (15 ml) ivory flat latex paint	2 drops burnt sienna
	1 tbsp (15 ml) ivory flat latex paint

Pour the buff, sandy glaze into a sealed container.

6. MOTTLING CREAMY-GRAY GLAZE

Apply the glaze to the wall area to be marbled, and lightly over the drawn-out mirror surround. Wet the sea sponge and then squeeze out all water, until it is just damp. Apply the glaze in loose brushstrokes with a decorator's brush. Work a section at a time if marbling a large area. Dab over the glaze with the sea sponge to produce a soft, mottled effect, ensuring there is not too much of a build-up of glaze over the drawn areas. Leave for 20 minutes, or until dry.

7. MOTTLING BUFF, SANDY GLAZE

Rinse out the sea sponge and squeeze out the excess water. Apply the buff, sandy glaze in the same way as the first glaze. The whole area will now be covered in the mottled stage of the limestone effect. Allow to dry.

8 PREPARING GLAZES FOR MARBLE DRIFTS

Make a glaze roughly two tones darker than the original buff, sandy glaze by mixing 4 drops yellow ocher, 2 drops burnt sienna and 1 drop raw umber tinter into the clear glaze in the sealed container.

Make a translucent, soft-ivory glaze by mixing 2 tsp (10 ml) of ivory flat latex paint with 2 tsp (10 ml) of acrylic scumble glaze, and a little of the original creamy-gray glaze. Cover the glazes until needed. Also have the original buff, sandy glaze ready.

9 BUFF DRIFTS

The drifts of mineral deposits in the marble are now applied. These are usually large tapering bands of color starting wide at the top and tapering down to a thinner line. To achieve a realistic effect, keep the number of drifts to a minimum. Add to the overall trompe l'oeil realism by working the color over the molded section around the mirror as well as any wooden molding. Working on one drift at a time, use a wide fitch to paint loose wavering bands of sandy buff glaze across the marbled area. Very lightly soften these with a hog-hair softener. Then while the glaze is still a little wet, brush over the lower or upper edge of each drift repeatedly in one direction, until subtle ridges or tidemarks start to appear.

10 DARKER BUFF EDGES AND TRANSLUCENT IVORY

Use a small fitch brush dipped in the darker buff glaze to loosely paint irregular lines on one edge of the marble drifts. Work one area at a time. Soften first with the hog-hair softener and then very lightly sweep the badger softener back and forth over the area to make the line look as if it is "sitting" in the glaze.

Add uneven bands of ivory above each drift and soften as before. Continue working in this way until you have built up the drift effect across the wall.

12 TROMPE L'OEIL DIMENSIONS

Use the Vandyke brown, yellow ocher, and white gouache or acrylics to mix up a mocha brown, a pale buff brown, and an ivory color. Add a little of the original glazes to these three colors to give them a better flow for painting and to make them tone in with the rest of the scheme. Use these colors to gradually build up the three-dimensional effect of the mirror surround by adding highlights and shadows to the different molded aspects of the underlying drawing.

11 SMALL FRESCO-LIKE FRIEZE

In a divided palette, mix some of the buff, sandy glaze with the vermilion, cobalt, and leaf-green gouache or acrylic to make three soft muddy tones. Use an artist's sable brush to paint these tones onto the flowers and leaves on the small frieze under the mirror. Work one section at a time applying the paint with the artist's sable brush and softening it with a hog-hair softener or soft varnishing brush. Gradually build up these colors, also using the darker buff glaze to paint in areas around the flowers.

13 FINISHING

Add any final details or added depth. Then mix a drop each of raw umber, yellow ocher, and burnt sienna tinters with 8 fl oz (250 ml) acrylic eggshell varnish, and varnish the whole area. Add a coat of clear eggshell varnish. Carefully peel away the masking tape and clean off any paint marks.

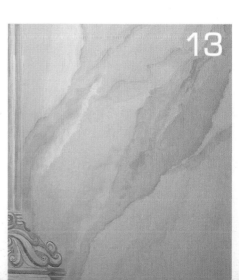

Naturals variations

Faux stucco squares and plaster mirror

Warm honey tones of classic polished plaster look beautiful. Prime and paint the walls with two coats of ivory flat latex paint. Cover with a taped grid at 12" (30 cm) intervals. Lightly varnish with acrylic eggshell varnish. Apply a coat of light beige flat latex paint in loose crisscross strokes. Mix a warm-beige glaze (use buff glaze recipe from Limestone marble trompe l'oeil, step 5, page 77). Apply to each square and stipple lightly. Add two drops of burnt sienna tinter and a little water to the glaze. Repeat the stippling process. Remove the tape. Paint a fine shadow line down and across one side of the grout lines in mocha brown. Varnish with acrylic gloss varnish. To make the mirror, stick ¹⁄₁₆" (2 mm) mirror glass onto a piece of ½" (12 mm) medium-density fiberboard. Mask off mirror then apply beige-tinted impasto. Varnish with one coat of acrylic matte varnish.

Pale gold damask

Here ivory and gold give subtle, reflective highlights. Prime and paint the wall with two coats of ivory flat latex paint and varnish with two coats of acrylic matte varnish. Stencil the first layer of the damask stencil on your chosen wall area, first in cream and then over-printed with pale gold stencil paint. Then apply the second-layer stencil in a creamy ocher (refer to Damask walls, step 4, page 42).

Travertine marble effect and decorative border

Create this cool floor for a sense of luxury. Prime and paint with two coats of ivory flat latex paint. Seal with acrylic eggshell varnish. Make guide marks for the border stencil. Create a taped grid inside them. Add tape for small diamond shapes at the joins of the squares, and triangles where the tiles meet the border. Mix a pale gray and buff-colored glaze (use recipe from Limestone marble trompe l'oeil, step 5, page 77). Apply a mottled effect over the whole floor. Make up an ivory and a darker buff glaze (step 8, page 78). Apply soft stripes on the large squares. Stencil the border with the ivory paint. Remove tapes. Paint fine edges to the border and grout lines. Varnish.

◄ The color scheme of your bathroom can be enhanced by the use of different accessories and ornaments. Here, the warm yellow of the bath and walls are complemented by gold picture frames, curtains, and a bronze statue, which give a sense of unity and coherence to the scheme.

► Even the smallest rooms can be transformed with some careful planning. The subtle textural contrasts of metallic squares on a matte surface have been used here to give light and extra dimension to this small space.

White to Gray

The white-to-gray palette gives both subtle and striking monochromatic possibilities with surprising versatility in style and effect, achieved by altering the proportions of white and shades of gray.

A predominantly white scheme will produce a clean, reflective, airy space, which stands in its own right or acts as a perfect backdrop for accents of contrasting or toning colors. A scheme comprising several tints of pale gray will create a light, yet truly neutral, restful feel. Combine pure white and gray tones for a contemporary look—ideal for abstract or geometric styles—or soften the palette by using pale ivory and blue-grays or green-grays for more traditional decorative schemes.

Use predominantly paler tints with accents of darker grays and charcoal to create a sophisticated scheme with lively contrasts and tonal variations; or try equal proportions of white and dark charcoal for highly contrasting, striking schemes that introduce a sense of formal elegance—particularly effective for stylish floors; silver metallic accents work extremely well with this palette.

Create the light, airy style of the northeastern seaboard in this **New England** themed bathroom.

New England style

Here the look is a blend of old-world charm and relaxed, contemporary living with a fresh, clean feel. Cool neutral whites and palest grays form the basis of the color scheme for wood paneling, painted walls, bathroom furniture, a bleached wood mirror frame and a monochromatic shoreline border, given extra definition with navy-gray check fabrics.

Where to apply

The walls here are a combination of painted flat walls and tongue-and-groove wooden paneling. Vary the proportions of paneling and painted walls to suit your bathroom, or cover all walls with either effect.

Difficulty level: moderate.

> ## Note
> Refer to page 40 for advice on constructing tongue-and-groove paneling.

Painted tongue-and-groove

New England is renowned for its wood siding painted in whites and light colors; here a subtle pale gray tone is used for this simple style of paneling.

PREPARATION

This project uses 4" (10 cm) V-joint tongue-and-groove paneling known as TGV. Once the wood paneling has been constructed, fill and sand any nail holes or cracks in the wood (refer to Damask Walls, page 40). Remove dust with a dusting brush. Apply stain-killing primer with a fitch brush to all visible knots, to prevent any discoloration from resin. Clean the brush with denatured alcohol immediately after use.

YOU WILL NEED:

4" (10 cm) V-joint tongue-and-groove timber (TGV) to cover the area to be paneled • wood filler • stain-killing primer • denatured alcohol • white acrylic primer • very pale gray flat latex paint • acrylic matte varnish • decorator's brushes • fitch brush • palette knife • sanding block • dusting brush

1 PAINTING

Prime the wood with one coat of white acrylic primer. Make sure that you push the primer into the V joins to achieve full coverage. Apply two coats of very pale gray flat latex paint to the paneled walls, allowing plenty of time between coats for the paint to dry out in the V joins. When the paint has fully dried apply two coats of acrylic matte varnish.

Shoreline Border

The soft gray theme is continued on the walls, with the addition of a band of ivory for the border stencil. The shoreline stencil is applied in a monochromatic palette, which creates a tonal, three-dimensional effect.

PREPARATION
Prime the walls with a coat of white acrylic primer and then paint with two coats of pale gray flat latex paint.

YOU WILL NEED:

Shoreline border stencil (page 121) • pale gray flat latex paint • ivory flat latex paint • white acrylic primer • acrylic matte varnish • stencil paints in ivory, pale gray, blue-gray, and dark blue-gray • repositionable spray adhesive • divided palette or paper plate • high-density foam in 1½" (4 cm) squares • paper towel • painting tape • masking tape • paint kettle • level • ruler • pencil • plastic eraser • permanent marker • hairdryer (if necessary) • tack cloth

MARKING UP STENCIL
Refer to Stencil Techniques (page 22). Draw a horizontal line onto the first layer of the shoreline border stencil ½" (1 cm) below the lower edge of the design. Then lay the second-layer stencil over the first, line up the motifs in the design, and trace the horizontal line. If the stencil does not have registration dots, check the motifs are still lined up and cut registration dots in the corners.

1 PAINTING BAND
Paint a band of ivory flat latex paint across the wall and make guide marks 9½" (24 cm) apart for the border. Stick painting tape along the marks, and seal with varnish.

Mix 1 tbsp (15 ml) of pale gray flat latex paint with 17½ fl oz (500 ml) of ivory flat latex paint and apply two coats to the band. Remove the top length of tape.

Stick painting tape ¼" (5 mm) above the lower tape, to make a thin line. Seal with varnish and paint with the blue-gray stencil paint. Remove the tapes and allow to dry. Varnish the walls with one coat of acrylic matte varnish.

3 ADDING DEPTH OF COLOR
Apply dark blue-gray paint to the tail feathers of the seagull on the highest post and all of the birds' beaks. Add highlights to the birds with ivory stencil paint. Make light pencil marks through the registration holes to position the next layer.

2 POSITIONING AND STENCILING FIRST LAYER OF BORDER
Spray repositionable adhesive onto the reverse of the stencil and secure to the wall. Pour some of the ivory, pale gray, blue-gray, and dark blue-gray stencil paints into a divided palette or onto a paper plate.

Use the pale gray lightly over the whole stencil, and then go back, overprinting the lower parts of the birds' bodies and the water. Use the blue-gray stencil paint to add more depth to some of the water, the wooden posts, the lower parts of the birds' bodies, and the tail feathers.

4 REMAINING REPEATS
Remove the stencil and reposition to the right of the first motif. Repeat the stenciling process. Refer back to the section you have just stenciled.

5 STENCILING SECOND LAYER OF BORDER

Spray repositionable adhesive onto the reverse of the second-layer stencil and position over the first layer, lining up the registration dots.

Use the blue-gray for the upper wing feathers and some details on the posts. Use the dark blue-gray for the remainder of the posts, the wings, and feathers, and to add depth to the beaks.

When the border is complete, varnish with two coats of acrylic matte varnish.

Cabinet and Mirror Frame

The painted wood theme is continued with a tongue-and-groove cabinet—painted in ivory and lightly distressed—and a rough timber frame, which is given a bleached, driftwood effect.

YOU WILL NEED:

Pine cabinet or other piece of furniture • rough pine frame and mirror glass • white acrylic primer • ivory wood paint or flat latex paint • acrylic matte varnish • stain-killing primer • denatured alcohol • decorator's brushes • fitch brush • sanding block • medium-grade sandpaper • masking tape • cotton • lint-free cloth • Plexiglas, or safe, shatterproof glass

PREPARATION

Refer to the guidelines in Preparation (page 14) for your particular cabinet. Sand the painted or bare surfaces thoroughly with medium-grade sandpaper to create a key. Apply stain-killing primer to any visible knots on bare or new wood to prevent any discoloration from resin. Cover any exposed hinges with masking tape.

1 PAINTING AND DISTRESSING THE CABINET

Apply one coat of white acrylic primer, making sure that paint is pushed into all the tongue-and-groove joins. Once the primer is dry, paint the cabinet with two coats of ivory wood paint, or ivory flat latex paint.

When the paint has completely dried use a piece of medium-grade sandpaper to distress the edges of the cabinet and cabinet doors. This will create a subtle distressed effect. Take care not to overdo this—keep the sanding minimal.

Finally, varnish with two coats of acrylic matte varnish. To add a finishing touch, apply the same treatment to the cabinet knobs.

For cabinets supporting sinks, protect the top with a sheet of shatterproof glass. Holes for sink plumbing should be made in cabinets supporting basin or bowl sinks before decorating. Use shatterproof glass to protect cabinets (a glazier should be able to cut out holes for plumbing).

2 BLEACHED EFFECT TO FRAME

Sand any rough edges off the frame and remove dust with a brush. Working on one side of the frame at a time, brush on the ivory wood paint or flat latex paint and wipe off immediately with a slightly damp cotton cloth, so that the paint stays in the grain, but is wiped away from the raised areas. Repeat on the three remaining sides of the frame. To make the effect more dramatic, repeat the process once the first coat of paint has dried.

This geometric repeat stencil creates a cool and stylish backdrop for modern fixtures and fittings, as well as mirrors and chrome accessories.

Geometric repeat

This design features a simple two-layer stencil. The gray and silver on white color scheme and bold shape of the stencil gives a really sleek, contemporary look.

Where to apply
Use on one wall or as an allover wallpaper effect for the whole room.

Difficulty level: **easy, as the design works on a square repeat basis.**

YOU WILL NEED:

Two-layer geometric repeat stencil (page 117) • white acrylic primer • soft white flat latex paint • acrylic matte varnish • acrylic eggshell varnish • stencil paints in pale gray, silver, and charcoal gray • decorator's brushes • repositionable spray adhesive • palette or paper knife • high-density foam in 1½" (4 cm) squares • paper towel • level • ruler • T-square • pencil • permanent marker • plastic eraser • tack cloth • hairdryer (if necessary)

PREPARATION
Prime and then paint the walls in soft white flat latex paint, taking care to create as smooth a surface as possible. Varnish the walls with one coat of acrylic matte varnish.

1 MARKING UP
Refer to Stencil Techniques (page 22). Use a level, ruler, and pencil to mark up horizontal registration guides at the top of the wall and to make vertical marks at the left edge of the wall. These marks will be important registration guides to keep the geometric design square while you are printing. Draw corresponding horizontal and vertical lines onto the stencil using a T-square and permanent marker.

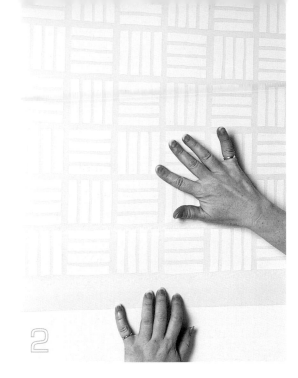

2 POSITIONING THE STENCIL

Apply repositionable spray adhesive to the reverse of the first layer of the stencil and secure the stencil in the top left-hand corner of the wall for the first repeat, lining up the horizontal and left-hand vertical registration guides. Ensure the cutout shapes are fully stuck to the wall to prevent bleeding. Refer to Stencil Techniques (page 22).

3 STENCILING THE FIRST REPEAT

Pour some of the pale gray stencil paint onto a palette or paper plate and apply using a piece of high-density foam. Stencil in light sweeping movements working in the vertical and horizontal direction of the design. Work from the top left-hand corner of the stencil to the bottom right-hand corner. If any patches of the stencil look a little transparent, overprint them with the same color to build up opacity. When the gray has dried, overprint the stencil using the silver stencil paint to give the first layer a metallic luster. Carefully peel the stencil away from the wall.

4 STENCILING THE SECOND REPEAT AND FIRST LINE

When the first repeat is dry (use a hairdryer if you want to speed the process up) position the stencil to the right of the first repeat. Make sure that the horizontal line at the top of the stencil lines up with the horizontal marks at the top of the wall, as well as positioning the left-hand side of the stencil so that the gap between the already printed motif and the new repeat is the same as in the design itself. In this way the design will have a continuous effect. Repeat the stenciling process using the pale gray and silver colors, moving to the right across the top of the wall, until the first horizontal row is complete.

5 COMPLETING THE FIRST LAYER

When the first line is complete, place the stencil under the first repeat, on the left-hand side. Ensure that the line on the left-hand side of the stencil lines up with the registration marks on the left-hand side of the wall, at the same time as positioning the top of the stencil so that the gap between the already printed motif and the new repeat is the same as in the design itself.

Stencil this repeat and then continue working from left to right until this row is complete as before. Continue this process until the first layer covers the whole of the area to be stenciled.

6 STENCILING THE SECOND LAYER

As soon as the first few repeats of the first layer are complete and dry, you can start working on the second layer in the top left-hand corner. This means that you can be working on both layers at the same time, and can move from one to the other while the stencil paint is drying.

Apply repositionable spray adhesive to the reverse of the second-layer stencil. Position the stencil by lining it up so that the smaller lines fit within the shapes of the first layer and do not overlap into any of the gaps. Stick the stencil securely to the wall to prevent any bleeding.

Stencil first with the charcoal gray stencil paint and when this is dry, go over it with the silver stencil paint.

7 REMOVING THE STENCIL

When you peel the stencil away, you will see that the second layer gives a pewter effect on top of the paler silver.

8 COMPLETING THE SECOND LAYER

Continue this process over all of the first-layer stencil motifs until all of the geometric shapes have the metallic ridged shape inside them. If you are stenciling a large area, you may find that the smaller cutout shapes in the second layer will become clogged with paint. If this is the case, remove the stencil and wash off the build-up of paint, dry the stencil and then continue printing.

9 FINISHING

Rub off any visible pencil marks and brush off any loose bits of eraser and then wipe over the whole surface using a tack cloth to ensure the surface is dust free. Finally varnish with two coats of acrylic eggshell varnish.

2 TAPING UP THE TILE GRID

Use the ¼" (7 mm) lining tape to create the effect of grout lines. Stick the tape around the inner edge of the border. Then measure 16" (40.5 cm) from the outside edge of two adjacent lines across the floor. Stick the tape on the outer edge of these marks to ensure the correct dimension; if the square is less than 16" (40.5 cm), the tape has been stuck on the wrong side of the line.

Mark up and stick down tape for the next two adjacent lines, measuring 16" (40.5 cm) from outside edge of last tape. Continue this process to build up a tiled grid. The last square may be cut short, but this will look quite natural, as the same thing would happen on a real floor. Seal tape with varnish to prevent bleeding.

3 MOTTLED MARBLE EFFECT

Starting farthest from the door, mask off the border with painting tape and seal with varnish. Then use the same technique to apply, mottle and soften the pale gray glaze from the Calacatta marble glazes to the whole floor area inside the masked-off border, working straight over the tape grid.

When dry, apply another layer of the pale glaze in the same way as the first. Allow to dry.

Tip

It is always best to start work on floors at the point farthest from the door and work toward the door.

4 CHECKERBOARD EFFECT

The checkerboard effect is achieved by applying a dark charcoal glaze to alternate squares. Use the lining-tape grid as a guide to mask off alternate squares, with the first dark charcoal square being in the corner that meets the marbled walls. Cut lengths of painting tape to mask off squares, trimming the ends.

Mix 7 fl oz (200 ml) acrylic scumble glaze with the pot of black flat latex paint. Add three drops of raw umber tinter, two drops of yellow ocher tinter, and equal amounts of acrylic eggshell varnish and water until the consistency is one of thick cream. Mix thoroughly.

5 APPLYING DARK GLAZE

The technique for applying this glaze is the same as for the pale glaze. Apply a second layer of this to create the depth of the dark charcoal. Dab a piece of scrunched-up plastic wrap to create a few lighter mottled patches.

6 LIGHT VEINS

Mix some acrylic scumble glaze, white flat latex paint, and a little pale gray glaze together to make a soft, translucent white.

Use a small fitch brush to paint small, random veins onto the dark charcoal and soften with the hog-hair softener. Vary the position of these veins square to square to create a realistic effect.

7 REMOVING TAPES AND FINISHING

Allow to dry for 20 minutes, and then carefully remove the painting tape and tape grid to reveal clear grout lines. Allow to dry thoroughly for at least 24 hours. Wipe over with a tack cloth, and varnish with two coats of acrylic eggshell floor varnish. Do not use for 48 hours.

White to gray variations

Shoreline mirror

This beautiful mirror frame is ideal for a sea-themed bathroom. Drill eight ¼" (6 mm) holes around the edge of ½" (12 mm) thick medium-density fiberboard measuring 15" × 18" (38 × 45 cm). Prime. Stick ⅟₁₆" (2 mm) thick mirror glass measuring 5½" × 7" (14 × 18 cm) onto the fiberboard. Mask off the glass. Paint the frame with pale gray flat latex paint. Paint several flat shells with white acrylic primer. Stick to the bottom of the frame, using tile adhesive. Stipple 3-D stencil paste or impasto around the shells. Remove tape. Stick ¼" (7 mm) soft white rope around the mirror with adhesive and seal edges with white (PVA) glue. Thread a 6½' (2 m) length of the rope through the holes in the mirror. Tie double knots in the rope and add white (PVA) glue.

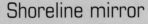

Abstract Oriental calligraphy on raised squares

Use this design to create an elegant and striking wall. Prepare, prime, and paint three 12" (30 cm) squares of ½" (12 mm) medium-density fiberboard and the walls with two coats of soft white flat latex paint. Seal wall and squares with acrylic matte varnish. Stick torn painting tape (refer to Soft vertical stripes, step 3, page 44) in a steep diagonal line on the wall, then onto the squares. Seal with varnish. Loosely paint and stipple a pale gray glaze (refer to Calacatta marble, step 1, page 92) to the right of the taped area. Stencil calligraphy motifs onto the squares in pale gray and charcoal. Overprint with pearl and silver stencil paints.

Koi carp etched glass

Create this beautiful, subtle etched-effect on glass—use on windows, mirrors, and the outside of shower screens or door panels. This is not a fully permanent finish. Clean the glass surface to be decorated with denatured alcohol. Stick your stencil securely onto the glass. Ensure good ventilation and spray several even coats of etching/frosting spray onto the glass. Leave for an hour, then carefully peel away the stencil (refer to Etched glass squares, step 5, page 53). Allow to dry fully.

► Marbling has been used on the side of this bath to give this neutral scheme extra interest and a look that is individual and classically elegant.

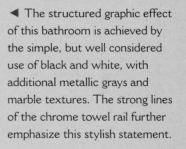

◄ The structured graphic effect of this bathroom is achieved by the simple, but well considered use of black and white, with additional metallic grays and marble textures. The strong lines of the chrome towel rail further emphasize this stylish statement.

Color Combos

The fascination with combining different colors in decorative schemes has been a strong influence throughout design history. Well-known principles of combining include polychromatic, harmonious, contrasting, and complementary schemes based on either synchronizing or contrasting color combinations (see Color, pages 24–25). Whether following established principles or simply working from instinct, color combining opens the door to a wonderful world of rich choices and diverse decorative possibilities. Further creative dimensions open up either by choosing pastel tints, bright colors, or deep shades; or by combining different color intensities and shades together. Try a palette that has two or three main colors, or else a scheme that has a predominant background color with added accents. Pastel combinations produce a light, yet crisp feel, as seen in the striped shower curtain project which has both harmonizing and contrasting elements; whereas bright polychromatic schemes give a lively, warm atmosphere, as shown in the Mediterranean bathroom, using primary colors, typical of that region. The Indian-style bathroom shows the richness of eastern influences in a predominantly one-colored palette with bright, contrasting accents.

These beautiful, soft-pastel stripes on pure white cotton voile have a clean, simple, and very modern feel, with a soft touch.

Striped shower curtain

This is used as an outer shower curtain to give a light, diaphanous, and airy feel to the bathroom.

Where to apply

This outer shower curtain is designed to be used with a waterproof shower curtain, which should be hung behind it. This treatment would look equally beautiful hung at the bathroom window, allowing the light to stream through.

Difficulty level: **this is a simple project, but the taping up and color sequence can be a little confusing at first.**

PREPARATION

To make up the shower curtain, first measure the area it will cover. If you are able to buy extra-wide fabric, simply add on 8" (20 cm) for hems at the top and bottom. If the fabric is too narrow buy enough for two lengths plus 16" (40 cm) for hems. If you are working with two lengths of narrow fabric, sew the seam of the curtain and then cut the width to size allowing 4" (10 cm) for the side hems. Pin a double 1" (2.5 cm) turning at the side edge and a double 1" (2.5 cm) hem along the bottom. Machine-sew and press. Pin a double 3" (7.5 cm) turning along the top edge. Machine-sew and press.

YOU WILL NEED:

100 percent cotton voile or cotton lawn in white to fit your shower curtain (usual dimensions 72" × 72" (183 × 183 cm) • large tabletop or counter • fabric stencil paints in pale creamy-green, pale turquoise-blue, light green, and pale sugar-pink • dressmaker's pins • sewing machine • sewing thread • low-tack masking tape in 2" (5 cm), 1" (2.5 cm), and ¼" (7 mm) widths • high-density foam in 1½" (4 cm) squares • sheet of bubble wrap • lining paper • divided palette or paper plate • paper towel • plastic bag or sheet of acetate • pencil • 6" (15 cm) plastic ruler • small strip of cardboard for marking up • scissors • fixings for hanging curtain (see Finishing, step 9)

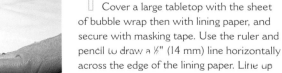

1

1 STICKING FABRIC TO TABLE

Cover a large tabletop with the sheet of bubble wrap then with lining paper, and secure with masking tape. Use the ruler and pencil to draw a ½" (14 mm) line horizontally across the edge of the lining paper. Line up the side-edge of the curtain with the line you have drawn and stick the fabric down so that the masking tape is exactly half on the table and half on the fabric. This will create a clean edge to the striped curtain.

2 TAPING WIDE AND NARROW STRIPES

Start by measuring 1" (2.5 cm) from the edge of the masking tape, making small pencil marks at intervals down the length of the fabric.

Carefully stick a line of 2" (5 cm) low-tack masking tape along the outer side of the marks you have made. Don't worry if it wrinkles a little. As long as the tape is securely stuck down, the end result will still be a straight line. Trim the edge of the tape so that it finishes right at the end of the fabric and does not stick onto the table.

To create the two thin stripes, measure ½" (14 mm) from the edge of this tape and make pencil marks at intervals as before and then stick down a line of ½" (14 mm) low-tack masking tape.

Measure a further ½" (14 mm) and stick down another line of 2" (5 cm) low-tack masking tape. Repeat the wide and narrow stripes until you have taped up the whole curtain.

Refer to the diagram below to help with the tape measuring.

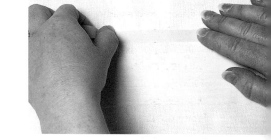

stripe space	tape	stripe space	tape	stripe space	tape	stripe space
1" (2.5 cm)	2" (5 cm)	½" (14 mm)	½" (14 mm)	½" (14 mm)	2" (5 cm)	1" (2.5 cm)

Tape layout

3 SPONGING PALE CREAMY-GREEN STRIPES

Pour some of the pale creamy-green, pale turquoise-blue, and light green fabric stencil paints into a divided palette. Dip a piece of high-density foam into the pale creamy-green fabric paint and dab off the excess on the paper towel. Wipe the pale creamy-green on the sponge over the first 1" (2.5 cm) stripe space to create the first pale creamy-green stripe.

4 SPONGING PALE TURQUOISE-BLUE STRIPES

Dip another piece of high-density foam into the pale turquoise-blue fabric stencil paint and dab off the excess on the paper towel. Wipe the pale turquoise-blue on the sponge over the two thin ½" (14 mm) stripe spaces to create the first thin, pale turquoise-blue stripes.

5 SPONGING LIGHT GREEN STRIPES

Now sponge the light green onto the next 1" (2.5 cm) stripe space to create a light green stripe. Once you have sponged in all of the stripes across the curtain, carefully peel back all of the tapes and discard. Allow the curtain to dry for up to an hour.

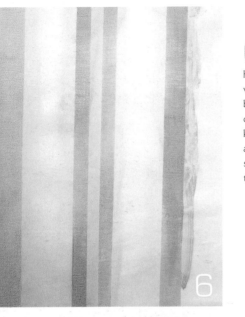

6 COLOR ORDER

The order that the colors are applied onto the curtain has been devised so that it takes four repeats of the stripes with the same colors, for example with the pale turquoise-blue to be used for the double-stripes. This gives the curtain much more interest, as the colors on the different widths of stripes keeps changing. Keep working in color order, regardless of the size of stripes and the color repeat will happen automatically. The pink is not used at this stage. The color order moving across the curtain is pale creamy-green, pale turquoise-blue, light green.

8 SPONGING SUGAR-PINK STRIPES

Pour some of the pale sugar-pink fabric stencil paint into the divided palette. Dip a sponge into the fabric stencil paint, dab off the excess on a paper towel, and sponge between the lines of masking tape.

7 TAPING FOR SUGAR-PINK STRIPES

Cut a strip of cardboard exactly 2" (5 cm) wide and draw two lines to make a ¼" (7 mm) band in the center of this cardboard. This will be used as a pattern to mark up the sugar pink stripes.

The sugar-pink stripes are placed between the pale turquoise-blue and light green stripes. Place the marked-up cardboard between these stripes and make two marks on the fabric that correspond with the two lines on the cardboard. As before, mark up at intervals along the length of the fabric. Repeat this process between each of the pale turquoise-blue and light green stripes. Stick two lines of 1" (2.5 cm) low-tack masking tape along these marks to make up the ¼" (7 mm) stripes.

9 FINISHING

Allow to dry for 10 minutes then remove the tapes. Lift the fabric off the table and hang to dry. Iron with a hot iron on the reverse side to fix the fabric stencil paints. To hang the finished striped curtain with your waterproof shower curtain, you can either use a grommet kit to make shower-curtain holes in the top of the fabric, or sew thin strips of voile to make tie-top headings, or use no-sew curtain clips.

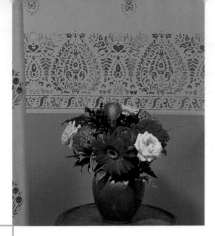

This themed project will allow you to bring the romantic and exotic opulence of India to your bathroom with rich, delicately patterned motifs, bright jewel-like colored walls and rich gold accents.

Indian-style bathroom

Follow these steps to create this exciting yet intimate look, for a space that will be perfect to unwind and wash away the cares of the world. The basic color combination here is the vibrant tones of pinks, oranges, and purples with gold accents. If this combination is too bright for your bathroom try using a similar combination but in pastel tones.

Difficulty level: moderate.

Where to apply

This two-layered stencil with its border and diamond repeat is ideally used with the border at the height of the sink, and the repeat pattern applied between the border and ceiling. It works equally well on silk and sheer fabrics, and the border would also be very attractive on a wide-framed mirror.

YOU WILL NEED:

Indian border and repeat stencils (page 122) • white acrylic primer • deep lilac-pink flat latex paint • paler lilac-pink flat latex paint • acrylic matte varnish • stencil paints in fuchsia pink, crimson pink, bright orange, and purple • metallic stencil paints in fuchsia, crimson, orange, yellow gold, pale gold, and purple • glitter stencil paints in gold and ruby • decorator's brushes • small fitch brush • repositionable spray adhesive • palette or paper plate • high-density foam in 1½" (4 cm) squares • paper towel • level • ruler • pencil and permanent marker • low-tack masking tape • painting tape

PREPARATION

Prime as necessary and then divide the walls into two sections at the height of the sink. Use a level to ensure the dividing line is horizontal. Paint two coats of the deep lilac-pink flat latex paint below the height of the sink. Once this is dry, mask this off with painting tape and paint two coats of the lighter lilac-pink from sink height to ceiling Once the paint is fully dry, varnish with two coats of acrylic matte varnish.

1 MARKING UP

Refer to Stencil Techniques (page 22). For the border stencil use a ruler and permanent marker to draw a straight line onto the first-layer stencil ½" (1 cm) below the lower edge of the design. This will act as a registration guide to line up to the line on the wall where the two different pinks meet.

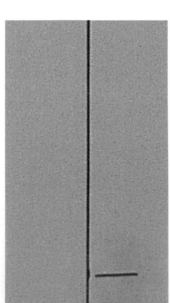

For the diamond repeat motif use the ruler and permanent marker to draw a vertical line running between each of the motifs on layer one of the stencil. Then use the level and pencil to make a series of vertical registration marks down the left-hand side of the wall. Refer to Stencil Techniques (page 22).

2 POSITIONING STENCILS

Apply repositionable spray adhesive to the reverse of the border and repeat stencils.

Stick the border stencil securely to the wall, with the registration guideline on top of the line where the two different pinks meet.

Stick the repeat stencil to the wall above the border stencil so that the edge of the stencil lines up with the registration marks on the left-hand side of the wall; also use the level to check that the vertical lines you have drawn are truly vertical.

3 STENCILING FIRST COLORS, FIRST REPEAT

Pour a little of each of the stencil colors into a divided palette or onto a paper plate.

The way of working the vibrant color palette in this pattern motif is to select different sections of the design for each color so there will be a section for the fuchsia and crimson pinks, a section for the orange and a section for the purple. This is then overprinted with the corresponding metallic colors. The pink colors should be prevalent, allowing the other two bright colors to blend and harmonize. You can devise your own system for this or follow the guidelines below.

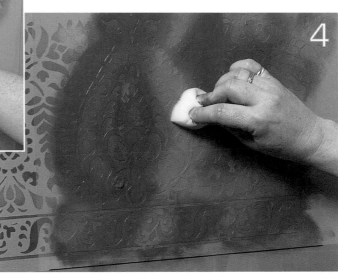

4 SUGGESTED COLOR LAYOUT FOR BORDER

Use the fuchsia and crimson pinks: on the left-hand side of the tulip shape in the pattern; to the left of the shape between the tulip motifs; for the centers of each of these two shapes; and for the S-shape and the linear shapes on the lower narrow border.

Use the orange to the right of the tulip motif: to the right of the shape between the tulip motifs, and between the S-shapes in the lower narrow border. Use the purple on the left of the inside of the tulip shape, the top of the tulip shape, the bottom of the shape between the tulip, and in any spaces left on the lower narrow border.

5 REPEAT-MOTIF REFERENCE

Use the fuchsia and crimson pinks for the top half (the flowers) of each motif.

Use the orange for the bottom half (the leaves) of each motif. Use the purple "blushed" around the edges of the flowers.

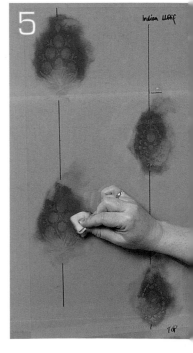

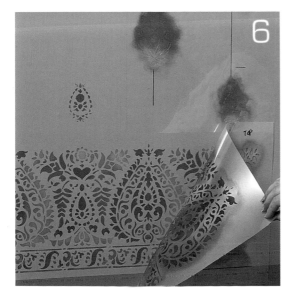

6 ADDING METALLIC COLORS

Metallic colors are naturally transparent and have little impact when put straight onto the wall. However, when they are stenciled onto rich base colors, as here, they will immediately have a lustrous depth. Stencil the corresponding metallic pink, orange and purple colors on top of the flat colors. Then add touches of the two golds to parts of the orange areas.

7 STENCILING REMAINING REPEATS

To reposition the border stencil for the rest of the border, make sure the guideline on the stencil is resting horizontally on the join line made by the two different pinks on the wall, as well as positioning the tulip motif at the left edge of the stencil so that it fits snugly into the last printed motif (the shape between the tulip shapes). Also ensure that there is the same amount of space between these two as there is between the motifs on the design itself.

You can either reposition the repeat stencil by eye, using the level to check that it is vertical, or by using a ruler to mark up the distance between each of the pattern motifs and line up to this.

Repeat the stenciling process using first the flat colors, followed by the metallic top color. Continue this process until the wall is covered.

8 GLITTER CENTERS

Apply repositionable spray adhesive to the reverse of the second-layer stencils for the border and repeat motifs and stick securely to the wall. Both of these stencils are easy to position by eye as they constitute the centers of the flowers and motifs for the first-layer stencils; just ensure that each shape is sitting inside its corresponding shape already printed and is not in any of the gaps.

This stencil will create the jewel-like, glittering centers to the flowers and shapes. It is done in two stages. First, use the gold glitter paint to stencil all the centers of the flowers and leaves on both the border and repeat motifs.

When this has dried, dab some of the ruby glitter paint onto your sponge and apply it directly to the stencil. To make the glitter paint stand out like little jewels apply a generous amount directly to the stencil with a small fitch brush.

Apply the ruby glitter paint to the center of the tulip shape, the heart, the pendant shape between the tulip motifs, and the central flower in the repeat motif.

Apply the gold glitter paint to the remaining centers. Peel back the stencil to reveal the beauty of these glitter centers.

9 FINISHING

A thin gold line is applied directly to the join of the two pinks to give extra definition and a metallic accent.

Measure ¼" (7 mm) up from the join line and mark it with pencil. Stick one length of low-tack masking tape onto the join line and another length on the marks you have just made. Press the tape down firmly by running your finger along each edge, brush over with matte varnish, and then apply two to three layers of gold acrylic paint using a fitch brush. Remove the tapes. Leave to dry until glitter paint has become hard, then use an eraser to remove any visible pencil marks, and brush off carefully.

The wall does not need another coat of varnish as two were applied on top of the base coat. Use a plastic eraser to remove any visible pencil marks and brush off.

The bright, sunny colors of Mediterranean interiors are captured perfectly in this simple, bold bathroom scheme, ideal for a room where you want a sense of warmth and invigoration.

Mediterranean floor

The polychromatic, primary color palette employed here is simple, yet highly effective. Create this tile-effect floor, which emulates the brightly colored, bold, simple patterns of thick Mediterranean ceramic tiles. Capture the floor colors in the walls for a really lively effect or complement the floor with pale, neutral walls.

Where to apply

This design works best as an allover floor treatment. It can be applied to a wooden floor, but will be most effective on a flat surface such as medium-density fiberboard or hardboard. The flooring is probably best laid by a professional, but if you are keen on DIY, refer to a comprehensive DIY manual to guide you through the relevant stages. You will need to work with sheets of ⅛" (4 mm) or ¼" (7 mm) thick medium-density fiberboard or hardboard.

Difficulty level: **moderate. The stencil is easy to work with, but floors are hard work so allow plenty of time for completing the project.**

PREPARATION

On wooden floors make sure the surface is well sanded; fill any holes with a proprietary wood filler. On medium-density fiberboard or hardboard floors also fill any holes made by tack heads with a wood filler and use an appropriate sealant to fill the sheeting joins. Prime the floor and then apply two coats of ivory flat latex paint. Allow to dry thoroughly, and then varnish with one coat of acrylic matte varnish.

MARKING UP FOR BORDER AND CORNER STENCILS

Refer to Stencil Techniques (page 22). Use a T-square to check if the line where the walls meet the floor is straight and square. Then, using the T-square, ruler, and pencil make a series of registration marks 2" (5 cm) in from the edge of the floor around the whole room, compensating for any unevenness in the walls and using the T-square to ensure 90° angles at the corners. These registration marks will act as guides for the border, corner, and tile stencils so spend time getting this right.

The border and corner stencils both have a linear motif at the base of the design. Use the permanent marker to draw a line directly onto the Mylar ¼" (7 mm) below this on both stencils.

1 STENCILING CORNER MOTIF

Pour some of the warm red, sunny yellow, and cobalt blue paint into a divided palette or onto a plate. Spray the back of the corner stencil with the repositionable adhesive and position the corner stencil so that the lines on the stencil line up with the registration marks on the floor.

Stencil the flower motif on the corner stencil lightly with the warm red. Then lightly dab a little blue in the center of the flower and stencil the linear motif around the edge in blue. Go over the flower again in red and then dab yellow into the small square in the corner.

Remove the stencil and repeat the process in each corner of the room.

2 STENCILING BORDER MOTIF

Spray the back of the border stencil with the repositionable adhesive and position so that the lines drawn on the stencil line up with the registration marks. Start the border next to the corner stencil.

Stencil the linear motif and the scallop motif in cobalt blue, the row of circles in sunny yellow, and the diamonds in warm red. Blush the top of the blue scallop motif with a little red. Remove the stencil and position again. Stencil as before. Repeat this process until you get to the next corner. On the last repeat you may need to stencil only a section of the border to fit in with the corner motif. To do this, simply mask off the area you do not want to print by laying a piece of paper under the Mylar and stencil as normal. Continue until the border is complete.

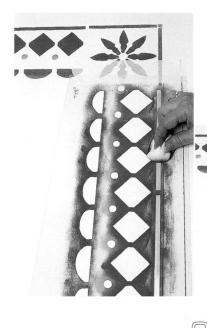

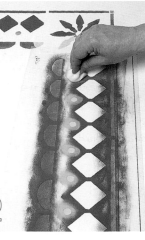

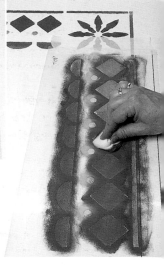

3 MARKING UP AND POSITIONING FIRST TILE REPEAT

Measure 5 ½" (14 cm) from the outside edge of the border stencil (linear motif) and make a series of registration marks to form a line inside the border all the way around the room. Use the T-square to make sure that the corners are 90°. Use the permanent marker, ruler, and T-square to draw a square onto the Mylar around the edge of the cutout motifs of the tile stencil.

Position the first tile repeat in the corner farthest from the door. The tiny triangle motif in the corner of the tile design should be closest to the corner stencil and the quarter-flower motif should be diagonally opposite.

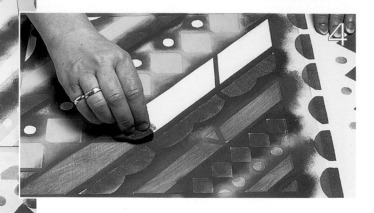

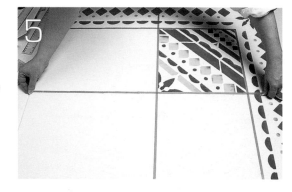

4 STENCILING FIRST TILE REPEAT

Working diagonally from the small triangle across to the quarter-flower motif, apply blue to the small triangle in the corner, the diagonal row of squares, the scalloped-lozenge shapes, and the single scallop shapes. Blush a little blue into the corner of the quarter-flower motif.

Stencil yellow to the short line of small circles, the diagonal row of larger squares, and the broken rectangles next to the quarter-flower motif. Stencil red to the three lines running diagonally across the tile, the longer row of circles, and the quarter-flower motif.

Some of the colors will naturally overprint. This adds to the ceramic glazed effect. To achieve color intensity, overprint the colors twice.

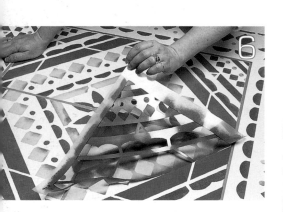

5 TAPING UP GROUT LINES

Stick lining tape along the marks already made (see step 3 above). Then make another series of marks to make up two lines adjacent to the corner of the room by measuring 11" (28 cm) from the outside edge of the first tape. When the tape is stuck down, check that the square measures 11" (28 cm); if it is smaller you have stuck the tape on the wrong side of the marks. Keep measuring and sticking down lining tape at intervals of 11" (28 cm) to make up a grid covering the whole floor. The last square will probably be cut short, which is exactly what would happen on a tiled floor as well.

6 STENCILING REMAINING REPEATS

The stencil is designed to be rotated 360°, to make up a full-pattern repeat. This in turn makes a series of square diamonds. In the center of one of these diamonds the quarter-flower motif lines up to make one large flower, in the other the repeat makes a series of concentric diamond shapes. The taped-up grid will help you position each repeat correctly. The square drawn on the stencil should fit perfectly inside the taped-up squares. Stencil the tile effect in rows, rotating the stencil 90°. Then rotate it back to the first position for the third repeat and so on. The second row you stencil will reveal the full pattern repeat.

7 APPLYING TINTED VARNISH

Tint 17 fl oz (500 ml) of acrylic matte varnish with five to six drops of raw umber tinter and mix thoroughly. Ensure the tapes are well stuck down and the surface is dust free. Varnish the whole stenciled area. Leave to dry.

8 REMOVING THE TAPES AND FINISHING

Peel back all of the tapes to reveal the crisp-edged grout lines beneath. Remove any pencil marks and wipe over the surface with a tack cloth. Finally, varnish the whole floor with two coats of acrylic eggshell floor varnish. Leave the floor varnish to harden for 48 hours.

Color combos variations

Oriental soft blossom

This delicate mural includes restful Oriental motifs. You can use any combination of Oriental-style stencils to make up the mural. Paint the wall with two coats of cream flat latex paint and acrylic matte varnish. Stencil—moon: gold; blossom: lilac, cerise, pearl; boughs: pale brown, gold; bamboo: pale gold; fretwork and calligraphy motifs: lilac, cerise, gold (refer to Dolphin backsplash, page 56).

Copper and silver

Here the simple combination of copper and silver creates a totally luxurious finish. The super non-absorbent surface of the copper paint is ideal for busy bathrooms, but extra care is needed in applying the paint to achieve a smooth surface. Refer to guidelines in Etched glass squares, page 52, for preparing and applying metallic paint. The contrasting silver effect is achieved by simply adding a gilded silver frame and brushed chrome fittings.

Scallop mosaic floor

This faux mosaic emulates traditional Roman floors. Prime and paint with two coats of white flat latex paint. Seal with acrylic eggshell varnish. Stipple a pale gray glaze over whole floor (refer to Calacatta marble, page 92). Make registration marks for the border. Stencil the corner and border motifs: pale gray, mid-gray, mid-blue, kingfisher blue. Add highlights: metallic blue, pearl, gold stencil paint/latex paint. Stencil the scallop motif inside the border using the same colors. Add two coats of acrylic eggshell floor varnish.

▶ Richly patterned walls create an opulent effect in this bathroom. This is further enhanced by the soft pinks of the floral motifs and bathroom fittings and the red wash on the lower walls. Fittings and accessories are kept to a minimum so as not to distract from the decorative features of the walls.

◀ This simple color scheme creates a sense of light and space— the perfect setting for showing off this roll-top bath, which takes center stage here. Further drama is created by light streaming through the large window—but even rooms without such direct light sources can be given a sense of light and space if the design and color scheme are carefully planned.

Stencil templates

Refer to Stencil Techniques (page 22) for instructions on how to cut and apply stencils. It may be worth enlarging the designs with a commerical copier. The stencils here can also be bought precut from www.hennydonovanmotif.co.uk.

Stencil designs copyright © Henny Donovan, 2003—may not be used for commercial purposes without prior permission of the author.

Level of difficulty

✳ Simple

✳✳ Medium difficulty

✳✳✳ Complex

✳✳✳ Damask walls

pages 40–43

Enlarge by approx. 300% for size shown in project • Two-layer stencil
The above diagram indicates how to position stencil for repeats to make the overall pattern.

pages 56-59 Dolphin mosaic backsplash and hand-painted tiles

Enlarge by approx. 300% for size shown in project

❇ Geometric repeat

pages 88–91

Enlarge by approx. 120% • Two-layer stencil

The diagram to the right shows how to make up the stencil design used in the project from the template below. Work with an even number of squares across the design to create a continuous repeat without needing to rotate the design.

☐ As template below

☐ Turn 90° counterclockwise

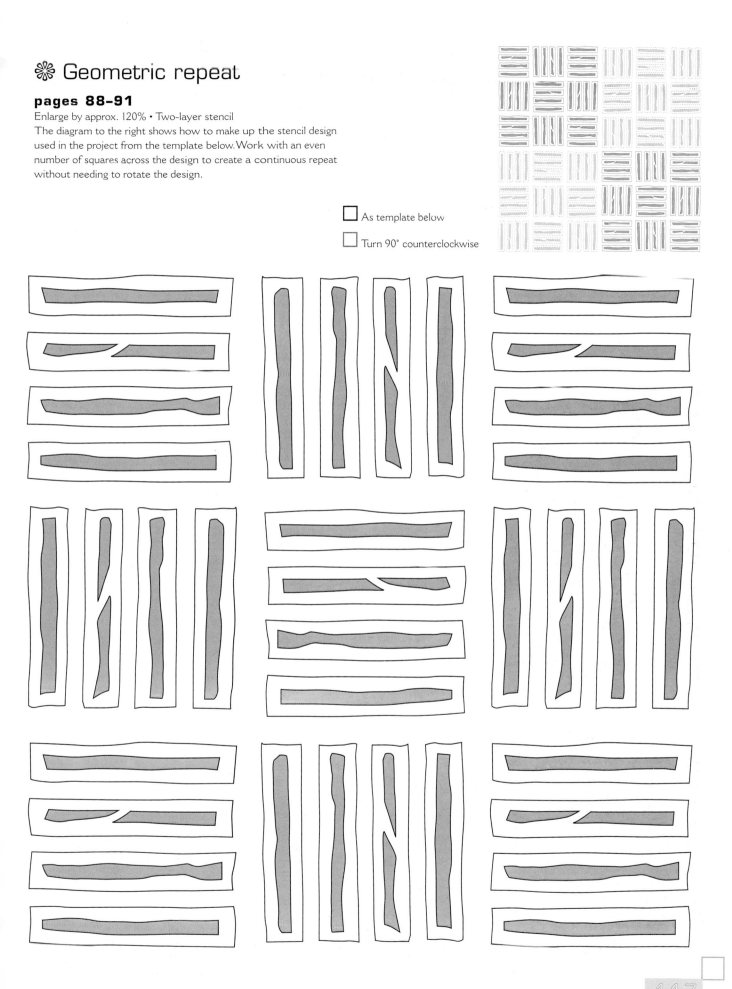

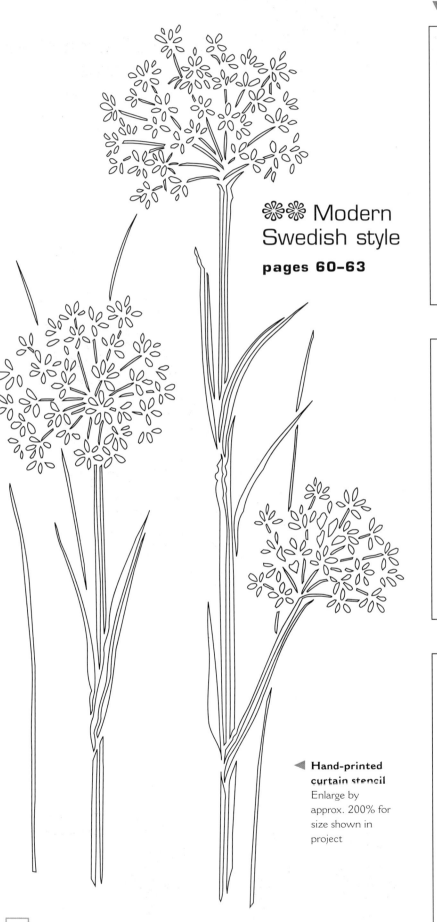

❀❀ Modern Swedish style

pages 60-63

◀ **Hand-printed curtain stencil**
Enlarge by approx. 200% for size shown in project

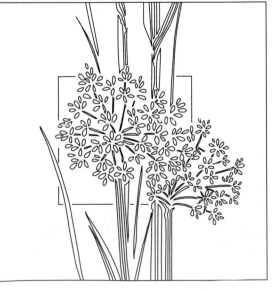

▼ Stencil guide for decorative squares

Enlarge by approx. 400%

✿ Etched glass squares

pages 52–55

Enlarge by approx. 150% for size shown in project

▼ Tile stencil

✿ Leaf spatter

pages 64–67

Enlarge by approx. 200% for size shown in project
Two-layer stencils

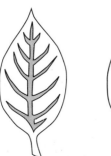

◄ Mirror frame border stencil

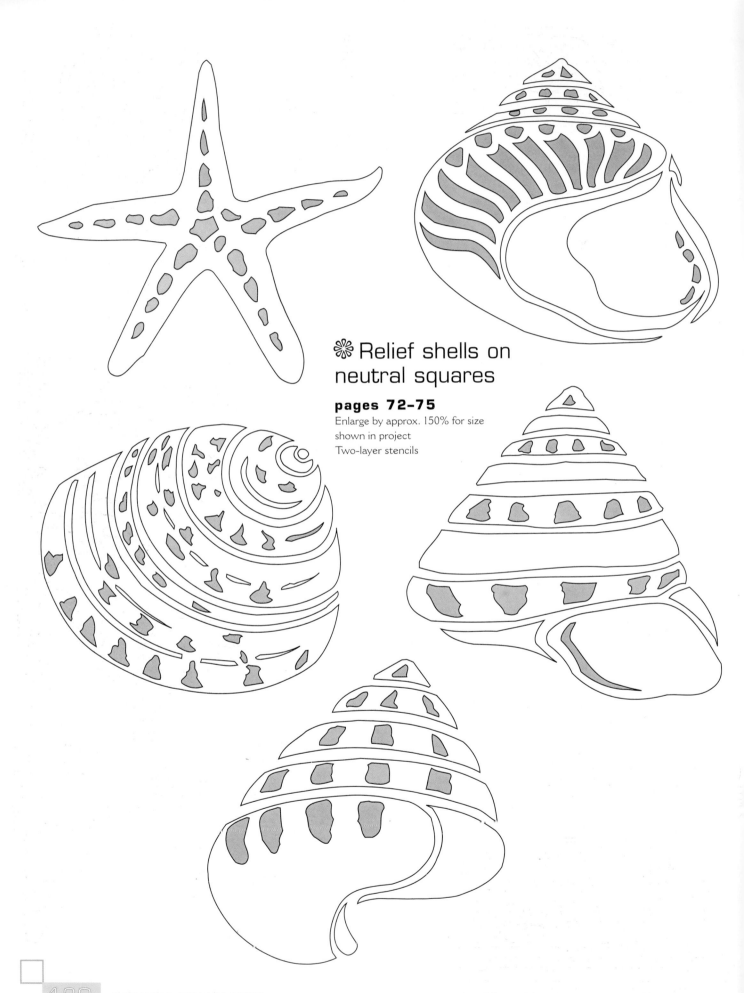

✳ Relief shells on neutral squares

pages 72–75

Enlarge by approx. 150% for size
shown in project
Two-layer stencils

✳✳ Limestone marble trompe l'oeil

pages 78-79

Enlarge by approx. 300% for size shown in project

Refer to the project to see how to flip the traced template in order to create a symmetrical right-hand side to the design.

▶ **Border repeat**

✳✳ New England style

pages 84-89

Enlarge by approx. 200% for size shown in project
Two-layer stencil

◀ Border repeat

❋❋❋ Indian-style bathroom

pages 104–107

Enlarge by approx. 165% for size shown in project
Two-layer stencils

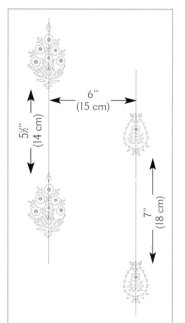

6"
(15 cm)

5½"
(14 cm)

7"
(18 cm)

▲ **Guide for wall motif repeats**

▲ **Wall motifs** ▶

▼ **Corner design for Mediterranean style**

✻ Mediterranean floor

pages 108–111

Enlarge by approx. 200% for size shown in project

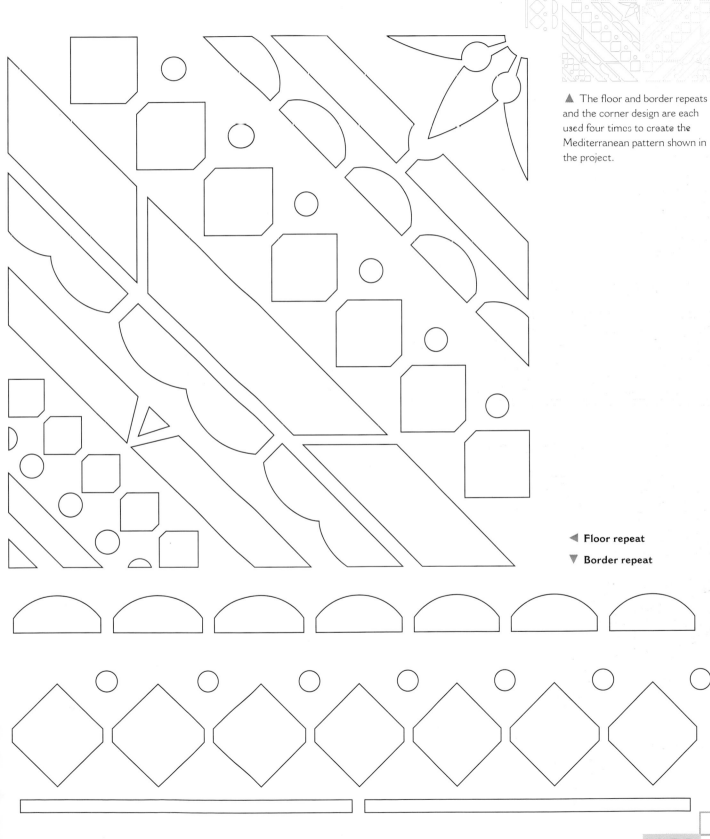

▲ The floor and border repeats and the corner design are each used four times to create the Mediterranean pattern shown in the project.

◀ **Floor repeat**

▼ **Border repeat**

Resource directory

The stencils used throughout the projects in this book, designed by Henny Donovan are available at www.hennydonovanmotif.co.uk. These include: Toile du Jouy, Large koi carp, Reverse feathers for etched effect, Dolphin mosaic, Reverse leaf for spattering, Wild parsley, Damask repeat, Modern shells, Geometric repeat, Shoreline border, Indian border, Indian repeat, Mediterranean tile, Dragonfly, Simple leaf, Mermaid and dolphins, Abstract oriental.

Also available: Decorative stencil paints, metallic stencil paints, glitter paints, 3-D stencil paste, porcelain paints, universal tinters, acrylic metallic varnish, acrylic varnishes, acrylic scumble glaze. Stenciling accessories, including high-density foam, specialist brushes, and tapes are among the range of equipment available. Go to www.hennydonovanmotif.co.uk for more information.

ABSOLUTE COATINGS INC.
38 Portman Road
New Rochelle, NY 10081
Tel (914) 636-0700
Fax (914) 636-0822
Web www.lastnlast.com
Varnishes and sealers. Information package available.

ADELE BISHOP
5575 N Services Road
Burlington, ON L7L 6MI
Tel (905) 319-0051
Fax (905) 319-0676
Web www.adelebishop.com
Precut stencils and art supplies.

ALBERT CONSTANTINE & SONS
2050 Eastchester Road
Bronx, NY 10461
Toll-Free 1-800-223-8087
Outside U.S. (718) 792-2110
Toll-Free fax 1-800-253-9663
Web www.constantines.com
Specialty decorating materials, crackle varnish, stencils, oil glaze. Also in Florida.

ART ESSENTIAL OF NEW YORK LTD.
3 Cross Street
Suffern, NY 10901-4601
Toll-Free 1-800-283-5323
Gold leaf and gilding tools.

ARTISAN SUPPLY CO.
5910 Arsenal
St Louis, MO 63139
Tel (314) 645-4795
Email fauxtools@aol.com
Web www.members.aol.com/fauxtools
Decorative painting tools, including stipplers, badger softeners, blenders, floggers, gilding brushes, and plaster blades.

BAYSIDE PAINT COMPANY
3603 Camino Del Rio West
San Diego, CA 92110
Tel (619) 487-6006
Fax (619) 688-0082
Web www.baysidepaintcompany.com
Variety of quality paints, brushes, and faux finishing products.

BEST LIEBCO CORPORATION
1201 Jackson Street
Philadelphia, PA 19148
Toll-Free 1-800-523-9095
Fax (215) 463-0988
Email bestliebco@aol.com

BLUE RIBBON STENCILS
26 S Horton Street
Dayton, OH 45403
Tel (937) 254-2319
Web www.blueribbonstencils.com
Over 90 precut stencils. Online retailer directory.

BRIWAX WOODCARE PRODUCTS
220 South Main Street
Auburn, ME 04210
Toll-Free 1-800-274-9299
24-hr fax line (212) 504-9550
Web www.briwaxwoodcare.com
Shellacs, varnishes, and wood waxes.

THE CHESHIRE CAT
538 3rd Street
Canmore, AB T1W 2J4
Tel (403) 678-3212
Web www.cheshirecatstencils.com
Precut stencil distributor. Wide variety.

CONSTANTINE'S
2050 Eastchester Street
Bronx, NY 10461
Toll-Free 1-800-223-8087
Fax (718) 792-2110
Metallic varnishes, gilding creams and waxes, white shellac, button polish shellac, gold leaf products.

DESIGNER STENCILS
c/o The Designer Shoppe, Inc.
3634 Silverside Road
Wilmington, DL 19810
Toll-Free 1-800-822-7836
Tel (302) 475-5663
Fax (302) 477-0170
Web www.designerstencils.com
Over 1100 precut stencil designs, including lettering, plus supplies.

DOVER PUBLICATIONS
11 East Ninth Avenue
New York, NY 10019
Tel (212) 255-6399
Reference books, period paints, ready-to-cut stencil designs.

DRESSLER STENCIL COMPANY
253 SW 41st Street
Renton, WA 98055
Toll-Free 1-888-656-4515
Fax (415) 656-4381
Web www.dresslerstencils.com
Over 300 precut stencil designs.

FINE PAINTS OF EUROPE
PO Box 419, Route 4 West
Woodstock, VT 05091
Toll-Free 1-800-332-1556
Fax (802) 457-1740
Web www.fine-paints.com
Importer of Schreuder high-pigment paints. Online retail directory.

FIRENZE ENTERPRISES, INC.
12976 SW 132 Avenue
Miami, FL 33186
Tel (305) 232-0233
Fax (305) 232-3191
Web www.rivesto-marmorino.com
Distributor of marmorino in 27 premixed colors, plus Italian-made trowels.

FROG TOOL COMPANY LTD.
2169 Route 26
Dixon, IL 61021
Tel (815) 288-3811
Fax (815) 288-3919
Paint strippers, brushes, varnishes.

FULLER-O'BRIEN CORP.
450 East Grand Avenue
South San Francisco, CA 84033
Toll-Free 1-888-681-6353
Web www.fullerpaint.com
Paints. Online dealer locator.

GOLDEN ARTIST COLORS, INC.
188 Bell Road
New Berlin, NY 13411-9527
Toll-Free 1-888-397-2468
Fax (607) 847-6767
Web www. goldenpaints.com
Artists' acrylic paints, retardants, mediums, and varnishes. Online dealer locator.

HOMESTEAD HOUSE AUTHENTIC MILK PAINT
95 Niagara Street
Toronto, ON M5V 1C3
Tel (416) 504-9984
Distributor of milk paint products. Call for color chart and retailer locations.

JANOVIC
771 Ninth Avenue
New York, NY 10019
Tel (212) 245-3241
Web www.janovic.com
Paints and specialist brushes.

KREMER PIGMENTS INC.
228 Elizabeth Street
New York, NY 10012
Toll-Free 1-800-995-5501
Fax (212) 219-2394
Web www.kremer-pigmente.de
Cadmium, natural earth, pearl luster, iron oxide pigments; metal powders, powdered stains, organic dyes.

L.A. STENCILWORKS
16115 Vanowen Street
Van Nuys, CA 91406
Toll-Free 1-877-989-0262
Tel (818) 989-0262
Fax (818) 989-0405
Web www.lastencilwork.com
Precut themed stencils, including
designs from Morocco, Italy, Mexico,
and Asia, plus supplies.

LEE VALLEY TOOLS LTD.
PO Box 6295, Station J
Ottawa, ON K2A 1TA
Toll-Free 1-800-267-8767
Toll-Free Fax 1-800-668-1807
OR
PO Box 1780
Ogdensburg, NY 13669-6780
Toll-Free 1-800-871-8158
Toll-Free fax 1-800-513-7885
Web www.leevalley.com
Shellac flake in white (clear), orange
(amber), garnet (deep red), and
other finishes. Mail-order and
Canadian locations.

**LIBERON/STAR WOOD FINISH
SUPPLY**
PO Box 86
Mendocino, CA 95460
Toll-Free 1-800-245-5611
Fax (707) 962-9484
Web www.woodfinishsupply.com
Wood finishing materials, paints and
varnishes. Online dealer locator.

THE MAD STENCILIST
PO Box 5497 Dept N
El Dorado Hills, CA 95762
Toll-Free 1-888-882-6232
Fax (916) 933-7873
Web www.madstencilist.com
Over 170 precut stencil designs.

**MOHAWK FINISHING
PRODUCTS INC.**
Route 30 North
Amsterdam, NY 12010
Tel (518) 843-1380
Crackle varnish, polishes, shellacs.
Atlanta, Dallas, California locations.

**THE OLD FASHIONED MILK
PAINT CO.**
436 Main Street
PO Box 222
Groton, MA 01450
Tel (978) 448-6336
Fax (978) 448-2754
Canada (416) 364-1393
Web www.milkpaint.com
Powdered milk paint in a wide range
of colors. Online dealer locator.

**PAINT AND DECORATING
RETAILERS ASSOCIATION**
403 Axminster Drive
St. Louis, MO 63026-2941
Tel (636) 326-2636
Fax (636) 326-1823
Web www.pdra.org
U.S./Canada trade association.
Online directory of paint and
decorative supply retailers.

PAINT EFFECTS
2426 Fillmore Street
San Francisco, CA 94115
Tel (415) 292-7780
Fax (415) 292-7782
Web www.painteffects.com
Decorative paint, decoupage, and
stenciling supplies, including colored
glazing liquid, craquelure, decoupage
lacquer, varnishing and antiquing
waxes, lining paste, brushes, tools,
and stencils.

PAINT MAGIC
412 Pebble Creek Court
Pennington, NJ 08534
Toll-Free 1-877-330-0445
Fax (609) 737-7333
Email pntmgc@aol.com
Web
www.desmondint.com/paintmagic
Prepared paint solutions including
colorwash, emulsions, glazing liquid,
craquelure, patina, impasto,
limewash, marmorino, primers,
distemper, and suede paint.
Canadian orders call for details.

PEARL PAINTS
308 Canal Street
New York, NY 10013
Toll-Free 1-800-221-6845 x 2297
Web www.pearlpaint.com
Paints and fine art supplies, including
metallic varnishes, gilding creams and
waxes, white shellac, button polish
shellac, gold leaf products, textured
gels, and dry pigments. Online retail
location directory.

**PERIWINKLE ESSENTIAL
STENCILS**
PO Box 457
West Kennebunk, ME 04094
Tel (207) 985-8020
Fax (207) 985-1601
Web
www.cybertours.com/periwinkle
Precut stencil patterns, including
botanical paintings, Delft pottery
patterns, and William Morris designs.

**PIEERE FINKELSTEIN
INSTITUTE OF DECORATIVE
PAINTING, INC.**
20 West 20th Street, Suite 1009
New York, NY 10011
Toll-Free 1-888-328-9278
Web www.pfinkelstein.com
European specialty brushes by mail
order.
Online catalog and order form

PRATT AND LAMBERT INC.
PO Box 22
Buffalo, NY 14240
Web www.prattandlambert.com
Paints, ready-mixed glazes and
varnishes. Online store locator; in
Canada call 1-800-289-7728.

**R & F HANDMADE PAINTS,
INC.**
110 Prince Street
Kingston, NY 12401
Toll-Free 1-800-206-8088
Fax (914) 331-3242
Web www.rfpaints.com
Hand-made paints, pigment sticks,
and encaustics. Online retailer
directory.

RENOVATOR'S SUPPLY INC.
Renovator's Old Mill
Millers Falls, MA 10349
Tel (413) 659-3773
General art supplies.

SEPP LEAF PRODUCTS
381 Park Avenue South
New York, NY 10016
Toll-Free 1-800-971-7377
Tel (212) 683-2840
Fax (212) 725-0308
Email sales@seppleaf.com
Web www.seppleaf.com
Gold and metal leaf, plus supplies and
tools. Gilding creams and waxes,
wood finishing and restoration
products. Kolcaustico Venetian
plaster. Metallic varnishes, white
shellac, and button polish shellac.

THE SIMS COLLECTION
24 Tower Crescent
Barrie, ON L4N 2V2
Tel (705) 725-0152
Fax (705) 725-8637
Web www.simsdesign.com
Precut stencils in whimsical designs.

SINOPIA LLC
229 Valencia Street
San Francisco, CA 94103
Tel (415) 621-2898
Fax (415) 621-2897
Web www.sinopia.com
Kremer pigments, metal powders
and filings, mica flakes, bronzing
powders, colored marble dust,
Venetian plaster, gilding materials,
specialty brushes, shellacs, waxes,
varnishes, acrylic glazing liquids.
Online catalog.

**STENCIL HOUSE OF NEW
HAMPSHIRE**
PO Box 16109
Hooksett, NH 03106
Toll-Free 1-800-622-9416
Tel (603) 625-1716
Web www.stencilhouse.com
Over 230 primarily floral precut
stencils, plus supplies.

STENCILS BY NANCY
15219 Stuebner Airline, Suite 5
Houston, TX 77069
Tel (281) 893-2227
Fax (281) 893-6733
Web www.stencislbynancy.net
Whimsical precut stencils.

THE TEXSTON COMPANY
8011 Webb Avenue
North Hollywood, CA 91605
Toll-Free 1-800-788-7113
Tel (818) 768-7676
Fax (818) 768-6773
Web www.texston.com
Veneciano, marmorino and terra
plaster products, available untinted
or tinted.

**WOODCRAFTER'S SUPPLY
CORP.**
PO Box 1686
Parkersburg, WV 26012-1686
Toll-Free 1-800-225-1153
Web www.woodcraft.com
Paint strippers and varnishes.

Index

Page numbers in *italics* refer to illustrations

A

accessories 28-9
acrylic varnishes 26-7
aluminum leaf 32-4, *32-5*
aquas 51-69
armoires 29

B

backsplash *13*
   dolphin mosaic 56-8, *56-9*
      template *116*
   leaf spatter 64-6, *64-7*
baths:
   choosing 28
   marbled side 97, *97*
   positioning *11*, 113
   roll-top *28, 63,* 113, *113*
bidets 29
bleach 18
blues 31-49
borders:
   shoreline *6, 7,* 85-6, *85-7*
      template *121*
bronze 81
brushes 20, *21*
   care 21, *21*

C

cabinets 29, 86
   preparation 16
Calacatta marble 92-4, *92-5*
ceilings: paints for 19
chairs 29
charcoal gray *6, 7,* 83
chrome 10, 71, *97, 97,* 112
collage: sea-theme 48, *48*
color *6,* 24-5
   combinations 25, 99-113
   cool and warm 24
   metallic 25
   mood and 8-9
   schemes 25
colorwashing 10
combing 10
condensation 14

copper 112, *112*
cream 71
curtains:
   hand-printed 62, *62*
      templates *118*
   shower: striped 100-2, *100-3*

D

damask effect 40-2, *40-3*
   pale gold 80, *80*
      template *114*
dampness 14
decorative scheme: planning 8-10
design:
   enlarging 37, *37*
   transferring 37, *37*
distressing 10, *10,* 69, *69,* 86, *86*
dolphins:
   and mermaid mural 68, *68*
   mosaic backsplash and hand-painted tiles 56-8, *56-9*
      template *116*
doors 12
   preparation 16
dragging 10
dragonfly motif 48, *48*
drawing equipment 20

E

environment 18
equipment 14, 20-1, *20*
etched glass:
   koi carp design 96, *96*
   squares 52-5, *52-5*
   templates *119*

F

fabrics 13
face-nailing *40,* 49
fantasy serpentine marble floor 68, *68*
faucets 29
faux etching 52-4, *52-5*
faux stucco squares 80, *80*
finishing 26-7

floors 13
   fantasy serpentine marble 68, *68*
finishes 27
   Mediterranean 108-10, *108-11*
      templates *122-3*
   mottled marble checker board 93-4, *94-5*
   paints for 19
   preparation 17
   raised 11
   sanding 17
   scallop mosaic 113, *113*
   travertine marble effect and decorative border 80, *80*
floral pattern 9, *9*
furniture 12, 29
   finishes 27

G

geometric pattern 9, *9*
   repeated 88-90, *88-91*
      templates *117*
gilding 27
gilt 71
glass 13
   etched glass squares 52-4, *52-5*
      templates *119*
   koi carp etched 96, *96*
   as protection 27, 38
glazes: applying 38
glitter paints 57
gold 71
grays *6, 7,* 31, 83-96
greens *7, 9,* 31, 51-69, 100-2, *100-3*

H

health 18
honey-beige 71

I

impasto 10
Indian style *8, 8,* 99, 104-6, *104-7*
   templates *122*
ivory 7, 71

K

koi carp etched glass 96, *96*
koi carp in silver aluminum leaf 32-4, *32-5*
      template *115*
koi carp and water lily mural 49, *49*

L

layout 11
leaf motifs 64, 65, *65,* 66, *66, 67, 68*
leaf spatter *13*
light: color and 25
lilac 31-49
linen presses 29

M

marble 6, 10
   Calacatta 92-4, *92-5*
   effect on bath 97, *97*
   fantasy serpentine marble floor 68, *68*
   limestone 10, 76-8, *76-9*
      template *121*
   mottled checkerboard 93-4, *94*
   travertine marble effect 80, *80*
marking equipment 20
marmorino 10
masking off 45
materials: for preparation 14
Mediterranean style 99, 108-10, *108-11*
      templates 122-3
mermaid and dolphins mural 68, *68*
metallic finishes 10, 52, 57
minerals 10
mirrors/mirror frames 29
   bleached effect 86, *86*
   plaster 80, *80*
   shoreline design 96, *96*
   silver *10*
   spattering 66, *66*
   stenciling 66, *66*
   trompe l'oeil 76-8, *76-9*
      template *121*
mixers 29, *29*
moisture 14

molding: adding 41
mood: creating 8-9
mosaic 10, *10*
    dolphin mosaic backsplash
        56-8, *56-9*
        template *116*
    scallop mosaic floor 113, *113*
motif pattern 9, *9*
murals 7
    koi carp and water lily 49,
        49
    mermaid and dolphins 68,
        68
    Oriental soft blossom 112,
        112
    seascape 36-8, *36-9*

N

naturals 71-81
New England style *6, 7, 8, 12,*
    84-7, 84-7
    template *121*

O

off-white 71
orange 31
Oriental calligraphy on raised
    squares 96, *96*
Oriental soft blossom 112, *112*

P

painting tape: tearing 44
paints 18-19
    glitter 57
    metallic 52
    porcelain 64
    spraying 46
    techniques 10
    textured 10
paneling:
    grey *6,* 84, *84*
    preparing 60, *60*
    tongue-and-groove 11, 12,
        40, 60, *60,* 84, *84*
pattern *6,* 9
    types 9, *9*
pictorial pattern 9, *9*
picture frames: gold 81, *81*
pink 31, 100-2, *100-3*
planning 8-10
plans: scaled 11, *11*

plaster:
    distressed 10
    with metallic finish 69, *69*
Plexiglas 27, *27*
porcelain liner 58
porcelain paints: preparing 64
preparation 14-17
primers 18, 60

R

racks 29
relief:
    shells *12*
        on neutral squares 72-4,
            72-5
        templates *120*
    stenciling 74, *74*
repeat designs 23, *23*
resource directory 124-5
rope spirals 48, *48*
rustic style 7

S

safety 18
sand color 71
sanding 17
scallop mosaic floor 113, *113*
sealants 18
sealing 26-7
seascape mural 36-8, *36-9*
Shaker style 12
shells:
    relief *12*
        on neutral squares 72-4,
            72-5
        templates *120*
shelves 29
shoreline designs:
    border *6, 7,* 85-6, *85-7*
        template *121*
    on mirror 96, *96*
shower curtain: striped 100-2,
    100-3
showerheads 29
silver 31, 32-5, 46, 71, 83, 112
    using 46
sinks 28
sketches 36, *36*
skirting board: adding 41
spatter 64, 65, *65,* 66, *66*
spirals:

rope 48, *48*
    stamping 69, *69*
sponging 69
spraying 46
squares:
    contemporary 49, *49*
    decorative 61, *61*
        templates *118*
    etched glass 52-4, *52-5*
        templates *119*
    faux stucco 80, *80*
    metallic 81, *81*
    Oriental calligraphy 96, *96*
    relief shells on 72-4, *72-5*
        templates *120*
stain-blocking primer 18
stamping: equipment 21
stenciling 6-7, *12,* 32-4, *32-5*
    damask 41-2, *41-2*
    equipment 21
    on fabric 62, *62*
    on glass 53, *53*
    relief 74, *74*
    techniques 22-3, *22-3*
    templates *114-23*
stone 10
stone color 71
storage units 29
stripes *13*
    effect of 9
    on shower curtain 100-2,
        100-3
    soft vertical 44-6, *44-7*
stucco lustro 10
styling 28-9
suede paint 10
surfaces 12-13
Swedish style *7, 12,* 60-2,
    60-3
    templates *118*

T

techniques 10, 12-13
templates *114-23*
terracotta shades 7
texture 10, *10,* 71
thematic approach *7, 8*
tiles 13
    baking 66
    finishing 66
    hand-painted 56, 58, *58-9*

Mediterranean tile effect
    108-10, *108-11*
    templates *122-3*
    mounting 66, *66*
    painting *13*
    stenciled tile effect *13*
tiling 11
toile du Jouy 49, *49*
toilet-roll holders 29
toilets 29
tongue-and-groove 11, 12
    painted 40, 60, *60,* 84, *84*
tools 20-1
toothbrush holders 29
towel rails 29, 97, *97*
towel rings 29
travertine marble effect 80,
    80
trompe l'oeil 29
    mirror frame 76-8, *76-9*
    template *121*
turquoise 50, 100-2, *102-3*

V

varnishes 26-7
ventilation 14

W

walls 12
    Calacatta marble 92-3,
        92-3, 95
    damask 40-2, *40-3*
        pale gold 80, *80*
        template *114*
    finishes 26-7
    flat painting 17
    paints for 19
    preparing 15-16
    soft vertical stripes 44-6,
        44-7
wash baskets 29
white *6,* 31, 83-97
woodwork 12
    finishes 27
    paints for 19
    preparation 16

Y

yellow 31, 81

Credits

Author acknowledgements and thanks:

Keith Bourdice for tireless support, encouragement, and help with set painting and construction. **Zoe Miller** for meticulous proofing and help with set painting. **Paul Forrester** and **Colin Bowling** for photography. **Sally Bond** for art editing and help putting my set designs together. **Kate Tuckett** for editing, project management, and sourcing props. **Jan Cutler** for copyediting. **Nikki Linton** for product sourcing. **Harriet Merry** for picture sourcing. **Sheila Volpe** for assistance with Damask stenciling.

The author and Quarto would like to thank the following companies for supplying props and supplies for photography:

Paint Magic Interiors for paints and varnishes used throughout the book

Brushstrokes (Cirka Wallcoverings) for Mylar and stencil paint used throughout the book

Bedec Products for specialist metallic emulsion

Pebeo Ltd for porcelain paints, stencil paints, gilding materials and stencil paste

John Jones for artist's materials and frames

Plasti-kote for etching/frosting spray and silver brilliant metallic spraypaint

Wm C Thomerson for discounts on timber, moulding and MDF, and for cutting all shapes and sizes

Fired Earth for loan of Bain de Bateau bath (p. 63) and Corinthian Stone Bowl (p. 79)

Bathstore.com for loan of taps used throughout, Calla frosted glass bowl with 600mm glass top (p. 35), bath and bath panel (pp. 39, 111), chrome shower head, chrome shower rail (p. 47), chrome towel rail (pp. 47, 75), chrome gallery shelf (p. 75), Muirfield 1 hole basin (p. 67), chrome gallery shelf (p. 67), Zero trough basin with chrome wrack soap dish (pp. 59, 95), chrome extendable bath rack (p. 85), Guido stainless steel basin (p. 91)

Colourwash for loan of cone basin (pp. 43, 87, 103)

Laura Ashley for loan of Venetian mirror (p. 43)

Next Mail Order for loan of glass shelves floor unit (p. 57) and round aluminium mirror (p. 55)

The White Co. for loan of towels and bathroom accessories used throughout the book.

Quarto would like to acknowledge and thank the following for supplying pictures reproduced in this book (key: l left, r right, c center, t top, b bottom): p. 6bl The Amtico Company Ltd. (www.amtico.com); p. 7tc The Dulux Media Centre at Ketchum, bathroom featured is Spanish Bathroom—BA2-WC (weww.ketchum.com); p. 8tl Fired Earth Ltd. (www.firedearth.com); p.11tc Utopia Furniture Ltd. (24-hour brochure line +44 1902 406405 or visit the website at www.utopiagroup.com); p. 24tl Utopia Furniture Ltd.; p. 28tl Albion Bath Co. (www.albionbathco.co.uk),tc Fired Earth Ltd., lc Fired Earth Ltd., rc Albion Bath Co., br Fired Earth Ltd.; p. 29tl Albion Bath Co., tc Fired Earth Ltd., tr Fired Earth Ltd., c Albion Bath Co.; p. 81t Utopia Furniture Ltd., b The Amtico Company Ltd.; p. 97t HK Art Projects (www.hkartprojects.co.uk), b Fired Earth Ltd.; p. 113 Susie Gradwell, b Abode Interiors Photography and Library (www.abodepix.co.uk); cover Abode Interiors Photography and Library